Winning Football with the

AIR OPTION Passing Game

Winning Football with the AIR OPTION Passing Game

Homer Rice
&
Steve Moore

Parker Publishing Company, Inc.
West Nyack, New York

© 1985 by

Parker Publishing Company, Inc.
West Nyack, N.Y.

Library of Congress in Publication Data

Rice, Homer.
  Winning football with the air option passing game.

  Includes index. 1. Passing (Football) 2. Football—Offense.
3. Football—Coaching. I. Moore, Steve
II. Title.
GV951.5.R5 1985 796.332'25 85-3593

ISBN 0-13-961038-3

Printed in the United States of America

Dedication

To Our Families

Our lovely wives and Head Coach of the families, Phyllis Rice and Carol Moore.

Our daughters and cheerleaders, Nancy Rice Hetherington, Phyllis Rice Ingle, Angela Rice Miller, Kimberly Moore, and Christy Moore.

The only son and future All-American, Steve Moore, Jr.

The grandchildren, Ryce, Leigh, and Drew Hetherington, Jamie Ingle, and Brian Rice Ingle.

FOREWORD

The air-option passing game is a continuation of the triple-option's offensive principles. If you read my book, *Homer Rice on Triple Option Football*, and comprehended the triple-pocket pass combination, you will have a better understanding of the implementation of the air-option attack.

After using the triple-option offense to establish a worthy record at the Universities of Kentucky, Oklahoma and Cincinnati, I was called to the athletic administrative level as Director of Athletics at the University of North Carolina. There I spent seven years building a total sports program at that great institution. During those seven years I continued to refine the triple-option, combining it with the pocket-passing game. Then the "call came," as we say in the coaching profession, to return to the "firing line" as Head Football Coach at Rice University, and later on as Head Coach of the Cincinnati Bengals of the National Football League. It was during both of these coaching positions that I had the opportunity to resume the air-option planning that has now spanned 30 years of my life.

During the seven years at North Carolina, I was often asked what offense I would employ if I should return to coaching. My answer was always the same— "the triple-option with the dropback passing game."

Therefore, at Rice University in 1976, we installed the 1968 Cincinnati Offense as our attack. We quickly learned two important lessons: (1) although sophisticated defensive coverages adjusted to the triple option, (2) no significant improvements defensed the dropback passing game. This lesson prompted us to design our offense to take full advantage of the defensive weakness. At the same time, a quarterback surfaced who fit perfectly into our thinking. Tommy Kramer not only molded into this concept, but he managed an unbelievable season in surpassing several N.C.A.A. offensive records leading the nation in total offense. Tommy was awarded consensus All-American honors and was drafted in the first round of the N.F.L. draft by the Minnesota Vikings.

Amazingly, the success of the air-option of 1976 equaled that of the triple-option pocket-pass combination of 1968. Much of the credit for the success should go to Steve Moore, a young assistant coach, who joined me at Rice University in 1976. Steve had gained his experience on the field as co-captain for

Coach Jack Curtice at the University of California at Santa Barbara. He had completed successful coaching careers at Temple High School, Temple, Texas under Bob McQueen; as Head Coach at Mesa Verde, Citrus Heights, California and as Quarterback/Receiver coach at the U.S. Military Academy at West Point. In 1978, Steve joined Coach Chuck Knox and helped turn the Buffalo Bills into the AFC Eastern Division Champions in 1980 and a playoff team the following year. In 1983, Steve moved with Chuck Knox to the Seattle Seahawks where they were part of one of the most dramatic turnarounds in professional football. It ended just one game shy of the Super Bowl. His knowledge, experience, positive attitude, and concentrated work habits will soon take him to a top coaching position. Steve Moore is joining me in co-authoring this manuscript.

HOW THE AIR OPTION CAN HELP YOU WIN

Our offensive philosophy is to develop the best of both worlds—a running game that attacks the defense and controls the ball when needed, and a passing game that exploits a wide-open but controlled attack. This offense could also be called upon in "catch-up" tactics if needed. This blend results with the triple option as our basic running game, and the pocket pass as our aerial game. Since we keep the ball in the air via the option pitch and/or the passing game with a variety of option keys, we label our offense the Air-Option.

Perfecting this combination will dissect defenses to your advantage, enabling your offensive unit to become highly successful. It is also great fun to coach, and the players enjoy the work habits necessary to implement the plan. In teaching this offense, the assignments are simplified in order to work primarily on technique. The simplicity of the offense enables the basis to be secured. However, we are flexible in order to prepare for any situation. The basic elements are adhered to before we add any flair, but our total thinking is simplicity with the sound basic techniques. Understanding and following a sound plan will bring about successful results.

It is important to determine your offensive philosophy. Through the many years of my coaching career, I was exposed to practically every phase of football in the football encyclopedia. Many times your talent and location shape your thinking, whether you develop a strong offensive running game or the aerial passing game. It is difficult to be strong in both, which means we must develop a philosophy of either run first or pass first. Whatever your decision, you, as the coach, must utilize 75 percent of the practice time developing that phase. I am convinced that if you understand completely the dropback passing game and have the ability to teach the air-option, you will have a distinct advantage over your opponents.

The air-option is exciting, producing fantastic results. It is a program possessing these ingredients: a team in top physical condition and highly disciplined; a sound, controlled defense; a potent kicking game; and an imaginative offensive plan, which will capture the fans' interest and make the coach a successful tutor. All the ingredients must be present. The air-option offense is stimulating to the teacher, to the participant and to the spectator.

This book presents primarily the dropback air-option passing game in complete detail. It is the first complete book on air-option principles. It is written for the football coach who has an interest in improving his profession, regardless of his area of interest—offense, defense, kicking game; for the skilled athlete who is so necessary for the air-option's productivity; and for the football fan who wants to become knowledgeable on an intricate phase of the game.

Homer Rice

INTRODUCTION

From its beginning the option running game in football has had consider-able success. The theory of two potential ball carriers attacking one defender with the option principle has had a dramatic impact on offensive philosophy. Example: Diagrams 1, 2.

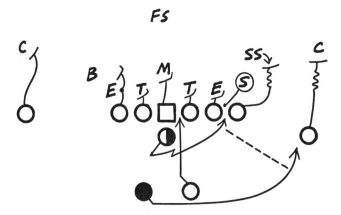

Diagram 1. Counter Dive Option

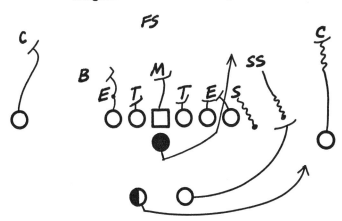

Diagram 2. Speed Option

The option design has three essential ingredients. First, the defender to be optioned must be isolated. Second, the two potential ball carriers must attack that defender with enough separation between them to make it impossible for the defender to stop both. The third essential is a correct option by the ball handler. The Air Option is a concept that incorporates these option principles into the design and teaching of a pocket passing game. By putting two pass receivers on one defender, the quarterback can option to the uncovered man and never be wrong. Example: Diagrams 3, 4.

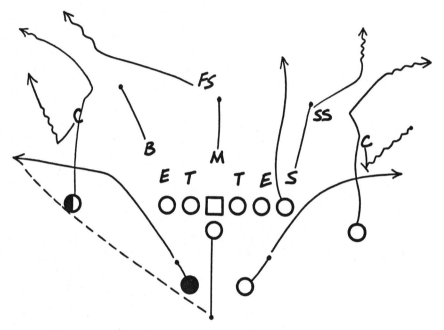

Diagram 3. Split End Drag and Halfback Flat Versus 2 Deep Zone

Just as the option running game is a complete run offense, the Air Option is a complete pass offense and can attack any pass defense. Its design has well-defined principles which make it easy for coaches and players to execute. It is a pass offense, not a collection of pass patterns, and it offers the players an unchanging plan which they can run over and over again to continually improve.

This book covers every aspect of the Air Option design. Formations, spacing, pattern design, the quarterback's option reaction, fitting patterns to coverages, protection, Air Option supplements, quarterback/receiver techniques and development in exact detail, and game planning are all reviewed. Although this design is uncomplicated, it must be executed precisely. The emphasis of the Air Option is on technique and consistency. The quarterback's drop and delivery must mesh with the pattern.

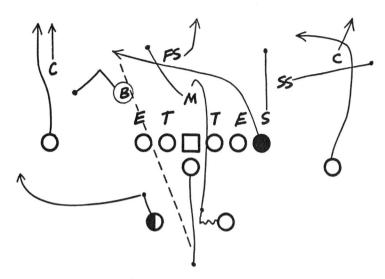

Diagram 4. Tight End Cross and Halfback Wide Versus
Strongside Zone

The design principles and techniques in the Air Option have been game
tested and found to be very productive. The theories result in steady progression
of skill development.

Homer Rice
&
Steve Moore

Acknowledgments

Susan Battles Phinney for her superb editing and preparation of this manuscript.

Elinor Moore (Steve's mother) for her work on the early stages of the Air Option.

Our coaching associates throughout the many years of a great profession.

The athletes who participated in the Air Option through the years to make this book a successful reality.

H.R. & S.M.

CONTENTS

Winning Football with the

AIR OPTION Passing Game

Chapter 1

A SYSTEM FOR
THE AIR OPTION

Before you dig into the actual plan of attack, it is important to formulate the nomenclature system. This chapter presents our organization for formations, spacing, alignment, numbering system, series, huddle mechanics, procedure at the line of scrimmage, cadence, audibles, and check-with-me. You need not change your system, but a classification of our organization will guide you through the design of the complete offense.

FORMATIONS AND SPACING

For a run-and-pass offense to complement one another, they should operate from the same offensive sets. The formations for the Air-Option passing game must force the defense to cover the width of the field. This has to be done without sacrificing the running game. Since a tight end and two running backs are required by most effective running games, the formation must get its width by deploying a wide receiver to each side of the formation (Diagram 1-1).

The formations are identified by two words. The first word describes the backfield variations: split, opposite, or "I." The second word (right or left) is the side of the tight end. All other players line up accordingly.

Against man-to-man or combination coverage, the spreading of the formation allows a full expression of the pass pattern. The defenders who are sprinting to cover their receivers, who are spread across the

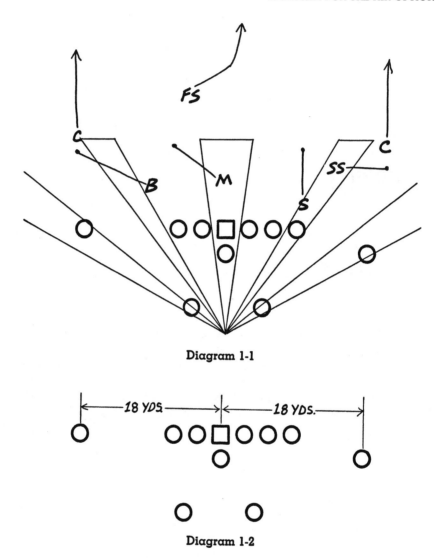

Diagram 1-1

Diagram 1-2

field, provide the quarterback with a distinct picture of the pattern and coverage. It becomes easy for him to spot the open receiver as he breaks from his defender.

The basic alignment for the wide receiver is approximately 18 yards from the ball. This will spread the defense nearly the width of the field (Diagram 1-2).

The 18-yard split by the flanker and split end is only the starting point in determining their exact alignment. Their actual alignment is determined by the quarterback's ability to throw the 17-yard out route. To stretch the coverage, the wide receiver should align as wide as possible. The stronger the passer, the wider the wide receivers can split. However, they should never align so wide that the quarterback cannot drive the ball to them on the out route.

Once the exact alignment is determined, it is best that the receiver stay with that alignment. In this way, he will provide a consistent target for the quarterback while keeping the coverage spread. A consistent alignment will also prevent the defense from keying alignment tendencies.

The necessary exception to this alignment is the 8-yard boundary rule that becomes a factor when the placement of the ball would force the receiver too close to the sidelines to run his outside routes. Never aligning closer than 8 yards to the sideline will allow the wide receiver to run any of his routes and catch the ball in-bounds (Diagram 1-3). There are also times that the wide receiver can slide his alignment to better support an offensive play. These alignment variations are game planned and should be kept to a minimum. If alignment variations are used significantly, it will be necessary to use decoy splits to break tendencies.

The basic alignment for the tight end places him 3 feet from his tackle. This is an adequate split for him to take an inside release on pass routes and still be in position to execute any of his blocks.

Proper interior line spacing is a very important part of the protection for the Air Option. The guards and tackles are split a full 3 feet (Diagram 1-4). They are also backed off the ball so that when they assume a three-point stance, their down hand will be 1 foot behind the neutral zone.

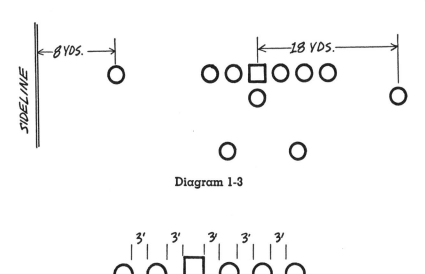

Diagram 1-3

Diagram 1-4

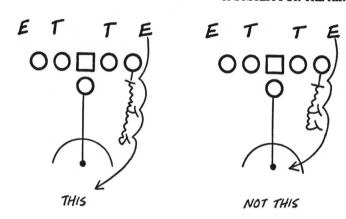

Diagram 1-5

With a seven-step dropback the quarterback's launch point will be 9¾ yards deep. Unless the line splits with enough width, the offensive tackles will not be able to bounce the contain rush around the throwing pocket (Diagram 1-5).

The alignment off the ball provides the linemen with a fraction of a second to set with strength and balance before taking on the pass rush. Also, this alignment will provide more time for the linemen to adjust to the various line stunts they will encounter.

Backfield Alignment

In the split back's set (Diagram 1-6), both backs align behind the inside leg of their tackle and with their toes 5 yards from the neutral zone. The opposite-back's set (Diagram 1-7) calls for the fullback to line up behind the ball with his toes 5 yards from the neutral zone. The halfback aligns the same as he did in split backs, behind his tackle. In the I-Back's set (Diagram 1-8), both the fullback and the halfback align directly behind the ball. The fullback lines up with his toes 5 yards from the neutral zone, while the halfback aligns with his toes 7 yards deep.

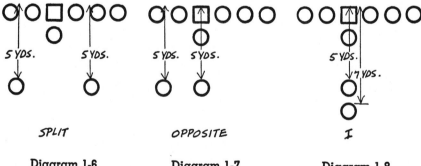

Diagram 1-6   **Diagram 1-7**   **Diagram 1-8**

NUMBERING SYSTEM

Hole Numbers for Running Plays—Strong side odd, weak side even (Diagrams 1-9, 1-10).

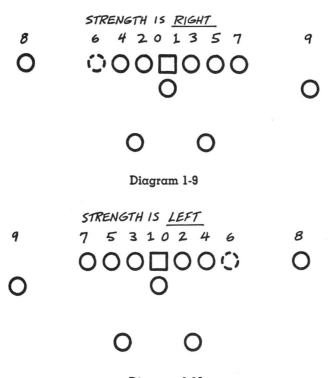

Diagram 1-9

Diagram 1-10

Ball Carrier or Receiver Identification Numbers (Diagrams 1-11, 1-12)

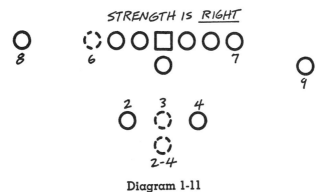

Diagram 1-11

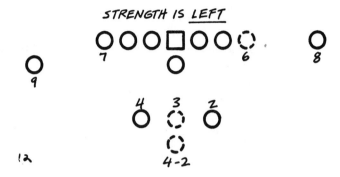

Diagram 1-12

Running plays are identified by a two-digit number. The first digit refers to the back who is to carry the ball, and the second digit indicates the hole where he is to run (Diagrams 1-13, 1-14).

Example: 34M (3 back, 4 hole, M blocking)

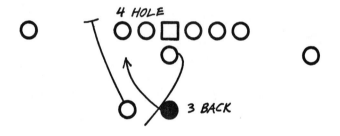

Diagram 1-13

Example: 38M (3 back, 8 hole, M blocking)

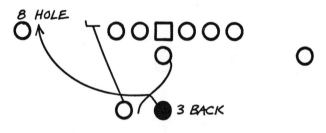

Diagram 1-14

Any blocking variations can simply be added onto the play number. (See Diagrams 1-15, 1-16, 1-17.)

Example: 27 Power (2 back, 7 hole, power blocking)

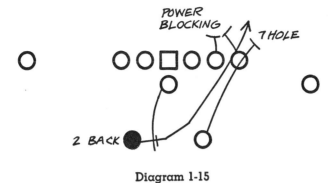

Diagram 1-15

Example: 23 Lead (2 back, 3 hole, lead blocking)

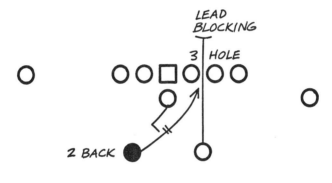

Diagram 1-16

Example: 29 Veer Option (2 back, 9 hole, veer option blocking)

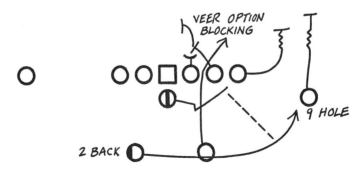

Diagram 1-17

Pocket pass plays are named with a two-digit number followed by two route names. The first digit refers to the protection series and the second indicates the primary receiver. The first route name is the route of the primary receiver. The second name designates the outlet receiver's route. All other receivers must learn their complementary routes. (See Diagrams 1-18, 1-19, 1-20, 1-21.)

Series are numbered:

50's: Quick pocket passes—quarterback three- to five-step dropback.

60's: Basic pocket pass—backs flare control, quarterback seven-step dropback.

70's: Fullback no pickup—quarterback seven-step dropback.

80's: Halfback no pickup—quarterback seven-step dropback.

90's: Both backs weak—quarterback seven-step dropback.

Route names:

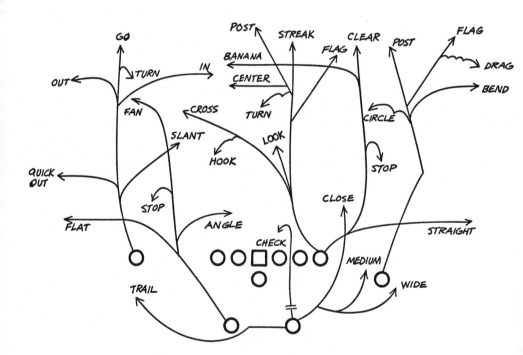

Diagram 1-18

Example: 69 In Hook (60 series, flanker in, tight end hook)

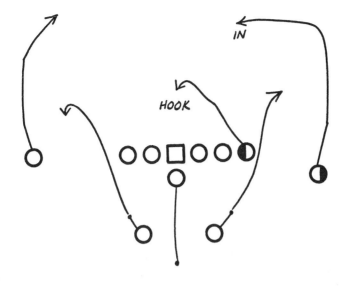

Diagram 1-19

Example: 67 Banana Angle (60 series, tight end banana, fullback angle)

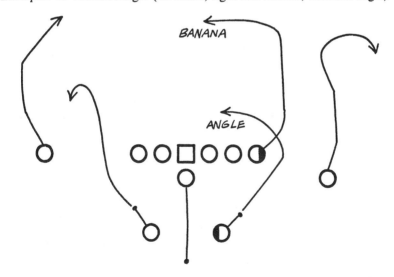

Diagram 1-20

Example: 92 Fan Tail (90 series, halfback fan, fullback trail)

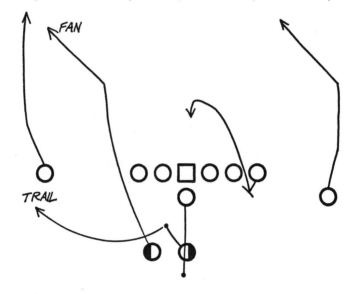

Diagram 1-21

HUDDLE MECHANICS

The center will set the huddle 8 yards from the line of scrimmage, directly behind the ball (Diagram 1-22). The rest of the team will line up as diagrammed, making sure to leave enough elbow room between them. Each player should be in a huddle stance with hands on knees.

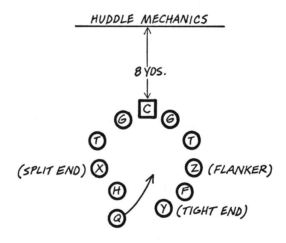

Diagram 1-22

Outside the huddle, the quarterback will survey the down, distance, and field position situation. After he has selected the play, he will enter the huddle and command "OK." On that command, his team members snap their heads up and direct all of their attention to the quarterback as he makes the call. They should focus their eyes on the quarterback's mouth to see as well as hear every word of the call. The call will be made only one time unless a player has difficulty hearing and is unsure of the formation, play, or snap count. At the completion of the call, that player says "check" and the huddle will be repeated.

The quarterback will call the running plays in this sequence:

1. Formation.

2. Ball carrier number and hole number that he is to run.

3. Blocking scheme or variation.

4. Snap count (with option to utilize pre-stance).

Example:

1. Opposite right—34 M on two.

2. Split left—46 Power on one.

3. Split right—28 Flip on quick from "up" (pre-stance).

The quarterback will call the passing plays in this sequence:

1. Formation.

2. Series number and primary receiver number.

3. Primary receiver's route name.

4. Outlet receiver's route name.

5. Snap count (with option to utilize pre-stance).

Example:

1. Opposite right—89 Drag—flat on three.

2. Split left—78 Hook—wide on the quick count.

3. Split right—79 Go—On three from "up" (pre-stance).

Each player should repeat the snap count to himself to lodge it into his subconscious mind. Once up to the scrimmage line, there will be defensive recognition, line calls, and audibles, all of which take concentration and may cause the player to forget the snap count. By concentrating on the snap count in the huddle, he will put it into his subconscious mind where later it will trigger his get-off on the right count.

When the quarterback has completed the huddle call, he will break the huddle with the words, "Ready . . . Break." All of the players should clap their hands simultaneously on the word, "break," and quickly move to their positions on the scrimmage line. On a left formation call, the backs will pause to allow the receivers to cross in front of them before moving to their assigned positions.

PROCEDURE AT THE LINE OF SCRIMMAGE

At the line of scrimmage, the team will quickly align in a three-point stance, unless the pre-stance is employed. By aligning in a three-point stance and utilizing the quick count a significant number of times, the offense will force the defense to declare its true alignment from the beginning. They will not be able to afford to align in a dummy front and get caught off-balance while trying to shift later in the cadence. The pre-stance allows the offensive unit to report on the line in an up position. If the snap count is on "quick," the ball will be snapped while the offensive linemen are in the up position. Should the snap count be called on a later count, the offense will go down in their three-point stance. The mixture of the up-and-down alignment continues to keep the defense on alert. They must be set, and, therefore, destroy their opportunity to disguise their fronts, stunts, and coverages. It also serves as an advantage for the pass blocker to be in the "up position" for protection on the quick count. When the team is set at the scrimmage line, the quarterback will put his hands immediately under the center (the defense must be ready when the quarterback is set), take a slight pause to identify the defensive front, and look for any alignment variation that may tip a coverage. After this pause, he will begin his cadence.

Example of cadence:

1. 43 Set
2. 1-28, 1-28
3. Hut—Hut—Hut

In phase one, the quarterback calls out the defensive front—"43" for example—to make certain that the offensive players are together in their recognition of the defense. Blocking patterns may change versus the different fronts—43, under, over, 34, etc. Although each offensive player is taught to see the front and make the needed adjustments, the call of the front ensures this.

In phase one, the quarterback will also call out "set," which is the quick snap count. Having a preliminary to the quick count (the front call) will prevent an offensive player from false starting when a defensive player makes a call soon after the team is set. This is a risk for teams that use the quarterback's first sound as their quick count.

The second phase is the audible phase. Either an audible or dummy call will be made. If an audible is needed, the quarterback will repeat the snap count called in the huddle and follow it with a new play. *Example:* Play called in the huddle—"opposite right-34-M-on *Two*." New Play called at the line—"43 Set, 2-38, 2-38." The new play to be run is 38 and will be run on the snap count that was called in the huddle—Two.

The quarterback should give the call first to the right side of the formation, "2-38," and then give it to the left side, "2-38." By always giving the call first to the right side, he will not fall into the habit of making his audible call first to the side of the new play and thereby tip the defense.

Some defensive teams will shift their front during this phase in an attempt to disrupt the audible system. By calling the snap count, "on the audible," the offense will catch the defense in the middle of their shift, thereby discouraging it. When the quarterback calls the snap count "on the audible," it will be snapped on the first single digit of the dummy call. *Example:* 43 Set, 2. The dummy call is made by voicing a number other than the snap count followed by the dummy play call. After a dummy call is made, the play called in the huddle will be run on the snap count that was called in the huddle.

This phase of the cadence can also be used for another method of calling the play at the scrimmage line—"check with me." In the huddle the quarterback will call the formation followed by, "check with me at the line," and then call the snap count. On the scrimmage line, he will survey the defense and then call a play in the same manner as he would an audible. This system of play calling is particularly useful versus teams that use a variety of defensive fronts or against a team that tips a coverage, line stunt, or linebacker dog. A high-percentage play can be called for the particular situation without the offensive players having to mentally shift from one play to another.

The third phase is the snap count phase. The ball will be snapped on one of a series of "huts" that is designated in the huddle. For example, if in the huddle the quarterback calls, "opposite right—34-M-on *Three*," the ball will be snapped on the third hut. The "huts" are nonrhythmical. The pause between the "huts" should vary to keep the defense off-balance. The quarterback can use this nonrhythmical count along with voice inflection to control the defensive charge. For example, if the ball is to be snapped on the third "hut," the pause between the first and second one can be medium length, followed by a higher-pitched and stronger hut. *Example:* "hut—*hut*—hut".

This should cause the defensive forcing unit to surge. As they shift back to regain their balance, the quarterback can call the third "hut" to catch the defense off-balance.

Another very important aspect of using the snap count as an offensive weapon, is on third down with 5 or less yards to go. The experienced quarterback can feel the tempo of the game and use the right pause with a sharp, loud "hut" to draw the defense offside to pick up a first down.

It is important the quarterback know that the defense will quickly disregard the sharp, loud voice inflection if it is used frequently. For this reason, it should be saved for eight or ten critical situations to help control the tempo of the game.

Chapter 2

AIR OPTION

PROTECTION SCHEME

THE protection rules for the Air Option are quite simple. They incorporate two basic principles.

First, there is a Big man on Big man rule—offensive linemen on defensive linemen. Offensive backs are assigned to linebackers. In this way, there should not be a big size mismatch for the offensive backs nor a mismatch in quickness for the offensive linemen.

Second, by assigning the running backs to linebackers, the scheme provides for maximum protection if needed. This also allows them to release into the pattern to help control undercoverage should the linebacker not rush.

For the purpose of simplicity of assignments, the defensive players are numbered. (See following Diagrams 2-1 through 2-6.)

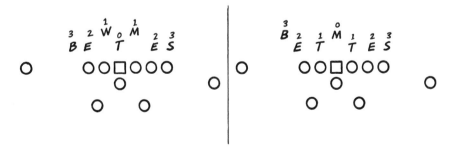

Diagram 2-1

50 PROTECTION (DIAGRAM 2-2)

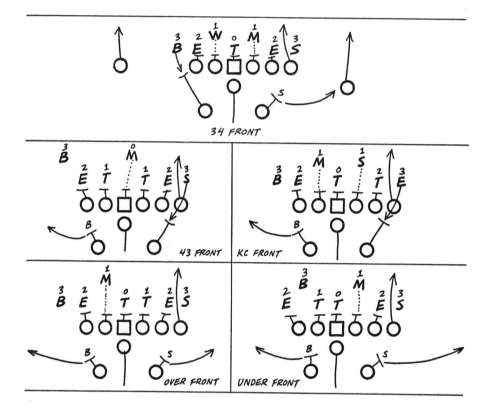

Diagram 2-2

Assignments

> *Center:* Number 0—linebacker or defensive lineman
>
> *Guards:* Number 1—linebacker or defensive lineman
>
> *Tackles:* Number 2
>
> *Fullback:* Number 3—flare
>
> *Halfback:* Number 3—flare
>
> **Note:** The quarterback will take just a three-step dropback. Linemen must set short and backs must take on their men near the LOS.

60 PROTECTION (DIAGRAM 2-3)

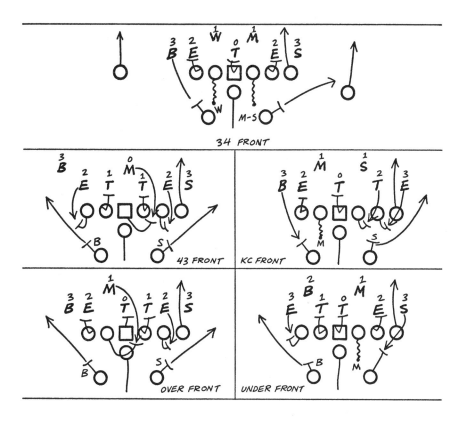

Diagram 2-3

Assignments

Center: Number 0—Linebacker or Defensive Lineman

Guard: Number 1—Linebacker or Defensive Lineman—Big man on Big man rule prevails versus KC front—slide

Tackles: Number 2—Big man on Big man rule prevails versus KC front—slide

Fullback: Strongside Linebacker—flare

Halfback: Weakside Linebacker—flare

70 PROTECTION (DIAGRAM 2-4)

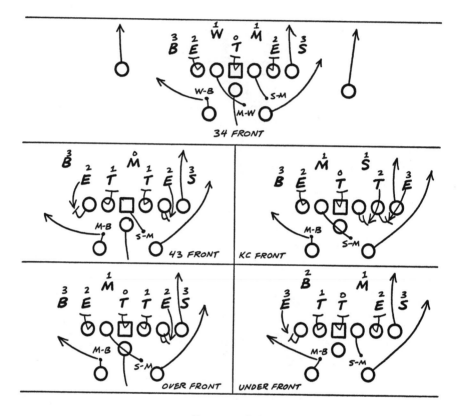

Diagram 2-4

Assignments

Center: Covered—Number 0/uncovered—combo linebackers strongside back

Strongside Guard: Covered—Number 1/uncovered—combo linebackers strongside back—Big man on Big man rule prevails versus KC front—slide

Weakside Guard: Covered—Number 1/uncovered—combo linebackers strongside back

Tackles: Number 2 Big man on Big man rule prevails versus KC front—slide

Fullback: No pickup—run route

Halfback: Combo linebackers strongside back—flare

Note: Uncovered linemen should come off the LOS 5 yards deep to combo linebackers.

80 PROTECTION (DIAGRAM 2-5)

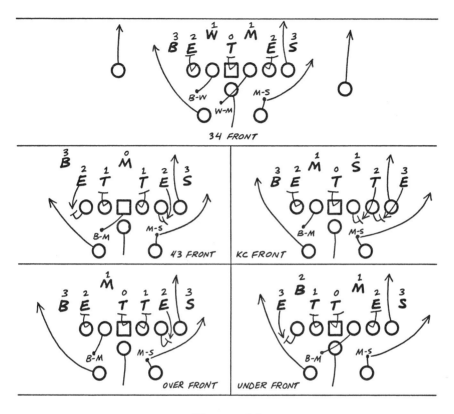

Diagram 2-5

Assignments

Center: Covered—Number 0 uncovered—combo linebackers weakside back

Guards: Covered—Number 1 uncovered—combo linebackers weakside back

Tackles: Number 2

Fullback: Combo linebackers weakside back—flare

Halfback: No pickup—run route

Note: Uncovered linemen should come off the LOS 5 yards deep to combo linebackers.

90 PROTECTION (DIAGRAM 2-6)

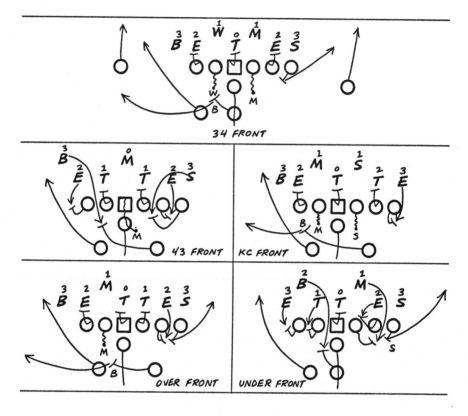

Diagram 2-6

Assignments

Center: Number 0—linebacker or defensive lineman

Guards: Number 1—linebacker or defensive lineman

Tackles: Number 2

Fullback: Weakside linebacker—flare

Halfback: No pickup—run route

Tight End: Number 3—flare

LINEMAN PASS PROTECTION TECHNIQUE

As was explained in Chapter 1, "A System for the Air Option," proper line spacing is a very important aspect in the protection-scheme. To provide the quarterback with an adequate pocket, the linemen must take 3-foot splits. This will allow the offensive tackles to reroute the contain rush outside of the throwing pocket.

The alignment off the ball (1 foot from the ball) will give the linemen a fraction of a second longer to set with strength and balance before having to take on the pass rush. This alignment also allows more time to adjust to defensive line stunts (Diagram 2-7).

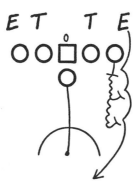

Diagram 2-7

The protection scheme for the Air Option assigns an offensive player to pass-block a defensive player man-for-man. There is a direct personal challenge. A key as to whether or not the offensive player is successful often depends upon his technique. It all starts with the proper stance. His stance must allow him to move on the snap with quickness and balance in a backward and/or lateral direction. This balanced stance is the same as the tight end or running back stance that is described in detail in Chapter 6, "Receiver Techniques for the Air Option."

If a guard or center is covered by a defensive lineman, he should set up on the line of scrimmage to take on his pass rusher. If there is a linebacker aligned on him, he will take a short step with his inside foot and then begin backpedaling straight backward. If his linebacker rushes, he will set up immediately to pick him up (Diagram 2-8). If his linebacker does not rush, he will continue backpedaling to a depth of 5 yards and set up ready to help on the first threatening defender (Diagram 2-9). An exception to this rule is the 50 Protection Series. Since the quarterback is dropping only three steps, the center and guard must set on the line. The offensive tackle's movement on the snap depends upon whether his guard has a defensive lineman aligned on him or not. If his guard is covered,

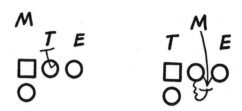

Diagram 2-8

Diagram 2-9

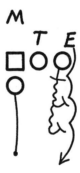

Diagram 2-10

he will take a short, quick step with his inside foot and then shuffle back and out to a position just inside the midline of the defender. At the same time, he will pivot to bring his shoulders at a 30-degree angle to the line of scrimmage between the defender and the quarterback's launch point. Whether it be a guard or tackle, this is the best possible position to protect the passer. From this position, he will set solid to execute his pass block and will shuffle only to maintain this relationship on his pass rusher (Diagram 2-10). If his guard is uncovered, the tackle should set as short as possible while sliding to this position on his rusher. This short set is to facilitate picking up line stunts and will be discussed later in this chapter.

To set up to take on his pass rusher, the lineman will snap to a fundamental football position with his eyes fastened to his target. The feet are just outside the shoulders and are even and point straight ahead. His weight is on the balls of his feet with the heels just off the turf. The ankles, knees, and hips are slightly flexed. The arms are slightly extended with the hands in front of the shoulders.

The actual block is more of a solid catch of the pass rusher than an aggressive attack. It is not nearly as important how hard the offensive lineman blocks as how long he blocks. He cannot be so aggressive that he gets overextended and thrown off-balance.

The block is made when the defender is near enough to make contact with and is made by the extension of the arms and a slight uncoiling of the hips and legs. The hands punch high up on the pass rusher's shoulder pads. The level of competition will determine the degree that the hands can be used.

From here the lineman maintains a solid press and fights to keep the best possible position to reroute the defender outside the throwing pocket. To do this, he must be able to shuffle to stay just inside the midline of the pass rusher with his shoulders perpendicular to the defender and the quarterback's launch point.

The shuffle must be done with quick foot movements that just skim the ground. One foot must stay on the ground as the other slides—he cannot hop.

The shuffle begins with the inside foot to the midline of the body. Next, he will push off with this inside foot and slide the outside foot to where the feet are just outside the shoulders once again (Diagram 2-11). This shuffle and press on the rusher continues until the quarterback delivers the ball. The offensive lineman must understand that his man-to-man challenge is often won or lost by a fraction of a second. For him to be consistently successful, the lineman must be willing to put forth his best effort to develop his pass protection skills.

Another phase of the lineman's pass protection technique is the picking up of defensive line stunts. The communication and feel that must be developed between the offensive linemen require a great deal of poise, concentration, and practice time.

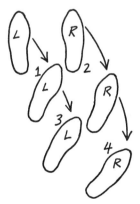

Diagram 2-11

There is a "best way" to pick up these stunts, based on the pattern as well as the angle of the defensive lineman's charge. However, rarely are these stunts as well defined as they appear on paper. It is in the gray areas that the feel and communication between linemen become so important.

This tackle-end stunt will almost always be manned (Diagram 2-12). The guard will set short on the defensive tackle. The offensive tackle will drop and then shuffle inside to meet the defensive end (Diagram 2-13). If, however, the defensive tackle aligns wide and on the snap forces the offensive tackle to take him, a switch call must be made by the tackle (Diagram 2-14). The angle of the defensive end's charge determines whether this tackle-end stunt is manned or switched (Diagram 2-15). If the defensive end takes a course through any portion of the offensive tackle, the tackle must set short and take him man-to-man. As soon as the guard feels the stunt, he will drop for depth and shuffle out to take the defensive tackle man-to-man (Diagram 2-16). If the defensive end aligns tight, or on the snap forces the guard to take him, a switch call must be made by the guard (Diagram 2-17).

These concepts apply to almost all other stunts when adjacent offensive linemen are involved. Regardless of whether it is a defensive lineman or a linebacker, the angle of the first defender's charge determines whether it is manned or switched (Diagram 2-18).

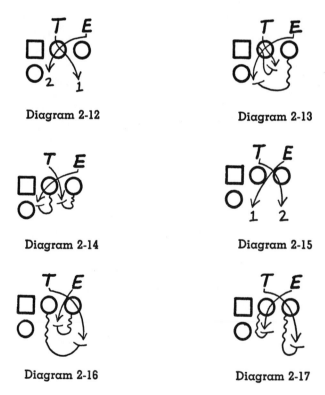

Diagram 2-12

Diagram 2-13

Diagram 2-14

Diagram 2-15

Diagram 2-16

Diagram 2-17

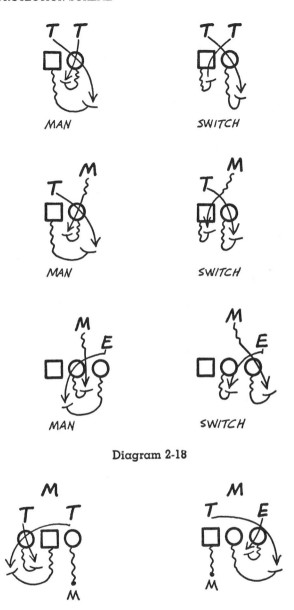

Diagram 2-18

Diagram 2-19

When a stunt crosses an uncovered offensive lineman (linebacker aligned over him), the communication will involve three people. The uncovered lineman will usually be involved in picking up the stunt, and the offensive lineman away from the stunt will assume his responsibility for the linebacker (Diagram 2-19).

RUNNING BACK PASS PROTECTION TECHNIQUE

On the snap, the back will take a jab-step with his inside foot, directly at his assigned linebacker. Should the linebacker rush, the back will continue in a very controlled run to meet his target. Once in position to make contact, his pass protection technique is the same as for the offensive lineman's that was just described.

Should the linebacker not rush, he will use his jab-step to spring him into his route. His protection responsibility is first, but the quicker he is able to recognize whether his assigned linebacker is rushing or not, the better.

Protection starts with recognition. When our linemen and backs know who to block, we then can spend more time in teaching how to block. This is the secret to offensive success.

The key is the teacher. I was always blessed with an outstanding offensive line coach: Owen Hauck at Highlands High School, Chuck Knox (Head Coach, Seattle Seahawks) and Bud Moore (Head Coach, University of Kansas) at the University of Kentucky. Barry Switzer (Head Coach, University of Oklahoma) at the University of Oklahoma, Ray Callahan (New York Jets) and Ralph Staub (Houston Oilers) at the University of Cincinnati, Charles Carr (University of North Carolina) and Ted Umbehagen (Texas Tech) at Rice University, Mike McCormack (Head Coach, Baltimore Colts) at the Cincinnati Bengals. Charlie Bradshaw, former Head Coach at the University of Kentucky, was one of the greatest teachers of offensive lineplay I was ever exposed to. His individual technique developments have been passed on to many. Ray Prohaska, Offensive Coordinator of the Seattle Seahawks, is the dean of NFL line coaches. His expertise in this area of the game is unmatched. Ray contributed to the chapter which again emphasizes the importance of the men in the trenches.

Spend important time developing the offensive line. It will pay huge dividends.

Chapter 3

DESIGN OF THE AIR OPTION

INCORPORATING QUARTERBACK OPTION

REACTIONS

THE pattern design of the Air Option places two receivers on one defender with enough separation between them to make it impossible for the defender to cover both. In theory, the quarterback simply options his pass to the uncovered receiver.

There are basic elements in this design. The first two elements serve to isolate the defender to be optioned, and the third creates the option by putting two receivers on the isolated defender.

First, the defense must be spread to restrict other pass defenders from helping the one who is to be optioned. This is done by aligning the split end and flanker with splits to spread the coverage and then patterning receivers to hold undercover defenders to their areas of responsibility. Second, there must be a clearing route to force the deep zone defender in the area of the pass to stay deep. He cannot be allowed to level and become a factor in the undercoverage. The third factor is to position receivers to front and back of the undercover defender to be optioned. The separation between these receivers must be enough to make it impossible for the defender to protect against both of them

The example in Diagram 3-1, diagrammed against a strong side zone coverage, has all three of these elements. First, the fullback and halfback hold the undercover defenders to their areas of responsibility by running stop routes.

Second, the split end clears the deep middle defender with a post route. Together, these receivers have isolated the MLB.

Third, the tight end fronts the SLB with an 8-yard hook route while the flanker backs the SLB with an 18-yard in route. There is too

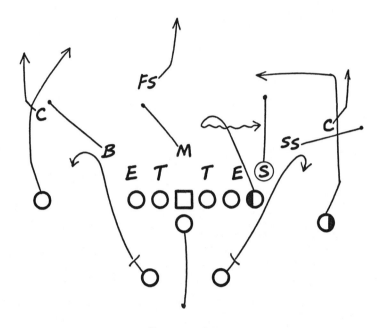

Diagram 3-1

much separation between the flanker and tight end for the SLB to defend against both. This creates the situation for the option.

The quarterback will option his pass to the uncovered receiver. His concentration is on delivering a timed pass to his primary receiver—the flanker running the in route. However, if the throwing lane is threatened because of a deep drop by the SLB, his reaction is to hit his outlet receiver—the tight end running the hook route.

Against man-to-man or combination coverages, the quarterback's option reactions remain the same. He will hit his primary receiver unless his receiver is unable to get enough separation from the defender. If the primary is covered, he options his pass to his outlet.

There is an added burden placed on the receiver versus man-to-man coverages. For the Air Option to be effective, the receivers must have the physical ability and developed techniques to consistently beat a man-to-man defender.

Not all of the Air Option patterns are designed with a clearing route in the area of the pass. Because of the deep threat that is built into the individual routes, and by virtue of the precise timing, many of the patterns do not require a clearing route. Now look at the following Air Option Diagram patterns (Diagrams 3-2 through 3-13), and the quarterback's option reactions versus several common pass defenses. It is important to know that the wide receiver routes are based on a specific number of steps. The complete description of these routes and their adjustments to coverages are found in Chapter 7 along with backfield and tight end routes.

69 IN-HOOK (DIAGRAM 3-2)

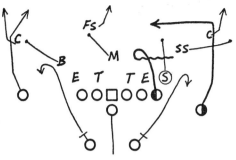

STRONG ZONE

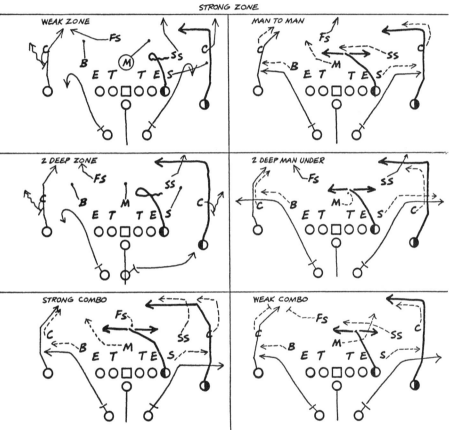

Diagram 3-2

Assignments

Split End: The split end runs a seven-step post route to clear the deep middle one-third defender.

Flankerback: The flankerback is the primary receiver. He runs a nine-step (16- to 18-yard) in route.

Tight End: The tight end is the outlet receiver. He runs an eight-yard hook route to front the defender responsible for the strongside hook zone.

Fullback and Halfback: The fullback and halfback have pickup on their assigned linebackers and then run stop routes. By running stop routes, they will hold undercoverage as well as be available to the quarterback as a trouble outlet. This route must be adjusted to flat route versus a man coverage. When aligned behind the center, the fullback adjusts his route to a medium route.

Quarterback: The quarterback takes a seven-step drop and delivers his pass to his primary receiver—the flankerback running the in route. Should the throwing lane to the flanker be threatened by a defender, he will option his pass to his outlet—the tight end running the hook route.

67 BANANA ANGLE (DIAGRAM 3-3)

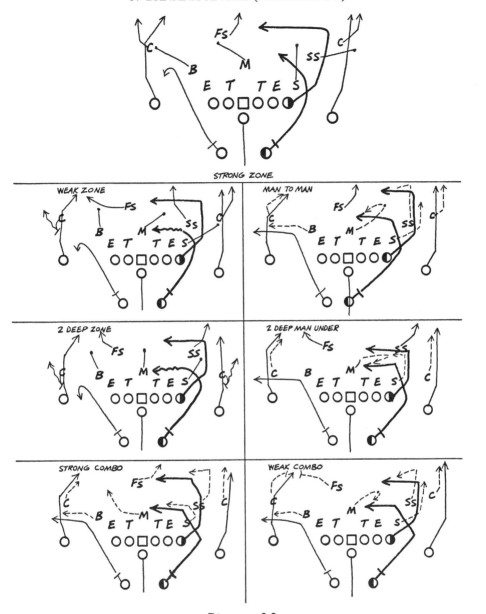

Diagram 3-3

Assignments

Split End: The split end runs a seven-step post route to clear the deep middle one-third defender.

Flankerback: The flankerback runs a go route to clear the deep outside one-third defender.

Tight End: The tight end is the primary receiver. He runs a 15-yard banana route.

Fullback: The fullback is the outlet receiver. He has pickup on his assigned linebacker and then runs an angle route. The angle route will front the defender responsible for the strongside hook zone.

Halfback: The halfback has pickup on his assigned linebacker and then runs a stop route. By running this stop route, he will hold undercoverage as well as be available to the quarterback as a trouble outlet.

Quarterback: The quarterback takes a seven-step drop and delivers his pass to his primary receiver—the tight end running the banana route. Should the throwing lane to the tight end be threatened by a defender, he will option his pass to the outlet receiver—the fullback running the angle route.

67 CROSS FLAT (DIAGRAM 3-4)

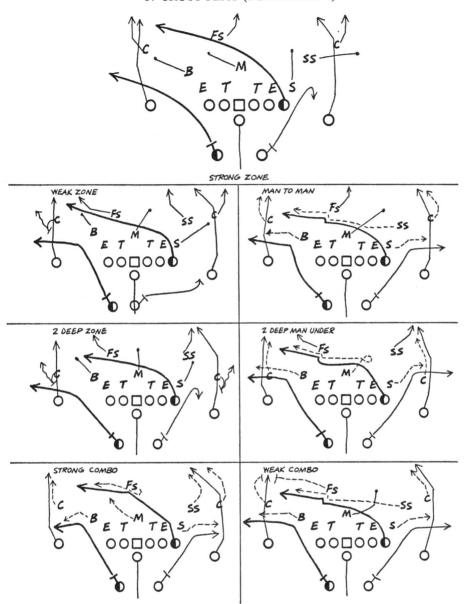

Diagram 3-4

Assignments

Split End: The split end runs a go route to clear the deep outside one-third defender.

Flankerback: The flankerback runs a seven-step post route to clear the deep middle one-third defender.

33

Tight End: The tight end is the primary receiver. He runs a cross route that puts him 17 yards deep in the opposite flat zone.

Fullback: The fullback has pickup on his assigned linebacker and then runs a stop route to be available as a trouble outlet.

Halfback: The halfback is the outlet receiver. He has pickup on his assigned linebacker and then runs a flat route.

Quarterback: The quarterback takes a seven-step drop and delivers his pass to his primary receiver—the tight end running the cross route. Should the throwing lane to the tight end be threatened by a defender, he will option his pass to his outlet receiver—the halfback running the flat route.

80 FAN TRAIL (DIAGRAM 3-5)

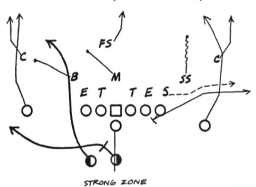

Diagram 3-5

Assignments

Split End: The split end runs a go route to clear the deep outside one-third defender.

Flankerback: The flankerback runs a seven-step post route to clear the deep middle one-third defender.

Tight End: First, the tight end has pickup on the end man on the line of scrimmage. If the defender does not rush, he will run a straight route to be available as a trouble outlet.

Fullback: The fullback is the outlet receiver. He has pickup on his assigned linebacker and then runs a trail route.

Halfback: The halfback is the primary receiver. He does not have pickup. On the snap, he runs a 17-yard fan route.

Quarterback: The quarterback takes a seven-step drop and delivers his pass to his primary receiver—the halfback running the fan route. Should the throwing lane to the halfback be threatened by a defender, he will option his pass to his outlet receiver—the fullback running the trail route.

88 HOOK TRAIL (DIAGRAM 3-6)

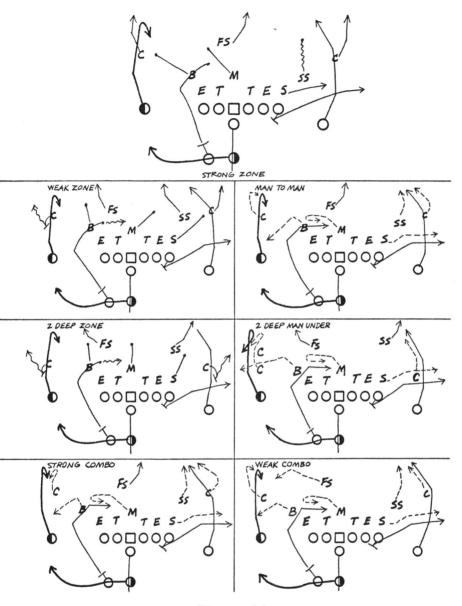

Diagram 3-6

Assignments

Split End: The split end is the primary receiver. He runs an eleven-step turn route.

Flankerback: The flankerback runs a seven-step post route to clear the deep middle one-third defender.

Tight End: First, the tight end has pickup on the end man on the line of scrimmage. If the defender does not rush, he will run a straight route to be available as a trouble outlet.

Fullback: The fullback is the outlet receiver. He does not have pickup. On the snap he runs a trail route.

Halfback: The halfback has pickup on his assigned linebacker and then runs an angle route. This route will hold undercoverage and make him available as a trouble outlet.

Quarterback: The quarterback takes a seven-step drop and delivers his pass to his primary receiver—the split end running the turn route. Should the throwing lane to the split end be threatened by a defender, he will option his pass to this outlet receiver—the fullback running the trail route.

69 DRAG WIDE (DIAGRAM 3-7)

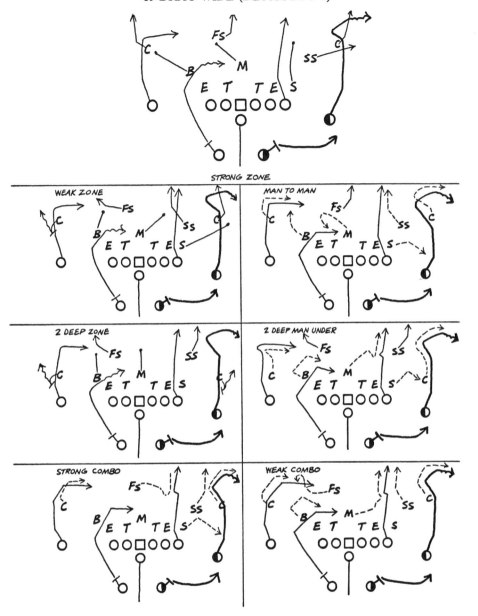

Diagram 3-7

Assignments

Split End: The split end runs an in-route.

Flankerback: The flankerback is the primary receiver. He runs a drag route.

Tight End: The tight end runs a streak route to clear the deep middle or deep half defender.

Fullback: The fullback is the outlet receiver. He has pickup on his assigned linebacker and then runs a wide route.

Halfback: The halfback has pickup on his assigned linebacker and then runs an angle route.

Quarterback: The quarterback takes a seven-step drop and delivers his pass to his primary receiver—the flankerback running the drag route. Should the throwing lane to the flankerback be threatened by a defender, he will option his pass to his outlet receiver—the fullback running the wide route.

69 CIRCLE WIDE (DIAGRAM 3-8)

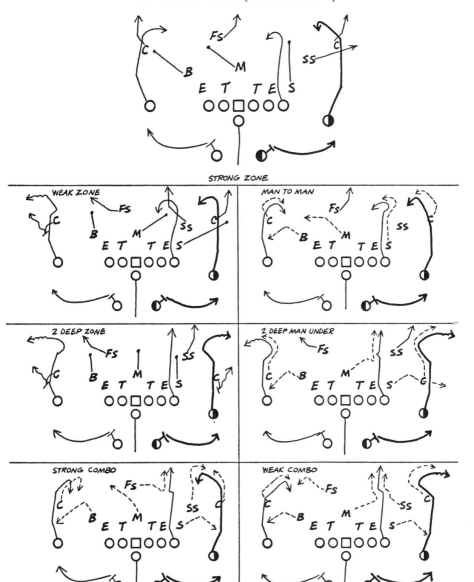

Diagram 3-8

Assignments

Split End and Flankerback: The receiver runs either a circle or drag route depending upon the coverage. Against rotation or invert type coverages, he will run a drag route. This is the best of the two routes for these coverages. He will run a circle route versus all other coverages. On 69 Read-Wide, the flankerback is the primary receiver and on 68 Read-Wide the split end becomes the primary receiver.

Tight End: The tight end runs either a streak or a turn route depending upon the coverage. If there is not a deep middle one-third defender, the tight end should give his undercover defender a shoulder-turn and then run a streak route. Against any coverage that has a deep middle defender, he will run a turn and be available as a trouble outlet.

Fullback and Halfback: The halfback has a pickup on his assigned linebacker and then runs a wide route. On 69 Read-Wide the fullback is the outlet receiver, and on 68 Read-Wide the halfback is the outlet.

Quarterback: The quarterback takes a seven-step drop and delivers his pass to his primary receiver—the flankerback running the drag or turn route. Should the throwing lane to the flanker be threatened, he will option his pass to his outlet receiver—the fullback running the wide route.

69 OUT-STOP (DIAGRAM 3-9)

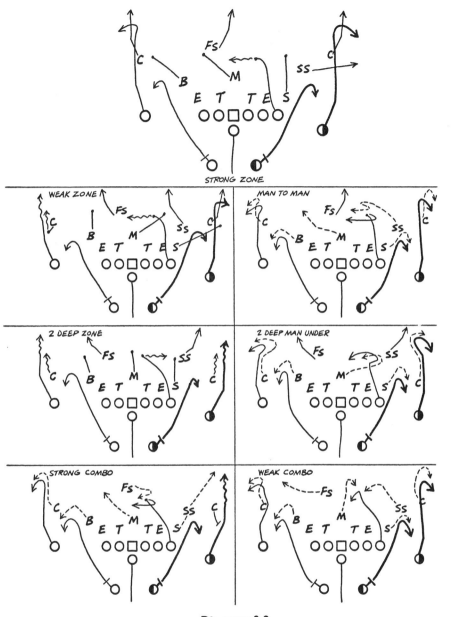

Diagram 3-9

Assignments

Split End and Flankerback: The receiver runs an out route. On 69 Out-Stop, the flankerback is the primary receiver and on 68 Out-Stop, the split end becomes the primary receiver.

Tight End: The tight end runs an 8-yard hook route to hold middle under-coverage and to be available as an emergency outlet.

Fullback and Halfback: The back has pickup on his assigned linebacker and then runs a stop route. On 69 Out-Stop the fullback is the outlet receiver, and on 68 Out-Stop the halfback becomes the outlet receiver.

Quarterback: The quarterback takes a seven-step drop and delivers his pass to his primary receiver—the flankerback running the out route. Should the throwing lane to the flankerback be threatened by a defender, he will option his pass to his outlet receiver—the fullback running the stop route.

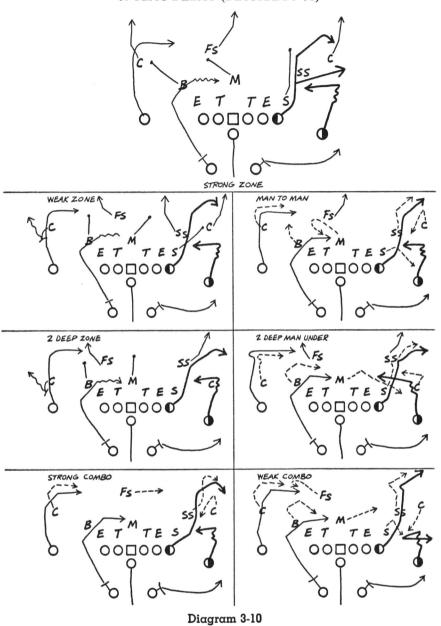

Diagram 3-10

Assignments

Split End: The split end runs an in route. This moving route combines with the halfback's angle route to give the quarterback a good trouble outlet pattern.

Flankerback: The flankerback is the outlet receiver. He runs a delay route.

Tight End: The tight end is the primary receiver. He takes an outside release and runs a flag route.

Fullback: The fullback has pickup on his assigned linebacker and then runs a wide route. He will provide the quarterback with a good trouble outlet.

Halfback: The halfback has pickup on his assigned linebacker and then runs an angle route. This route combines with the split end's in route to give the quarterback a good trouble outlet pattern.

Quarterback: The quarterback takes a seven-step drop and delivers his pass to his primary receiver—the tight end running the flag route. Should the throwing lane to the tight end be threatened by a defender, he will option his pass to his outlet receiver—the flankerback running the delay route.

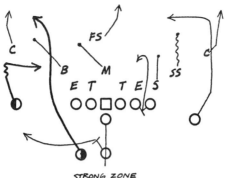

STRONG ZONE

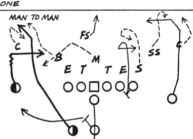

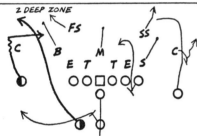

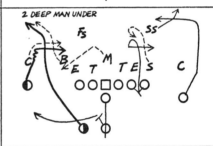

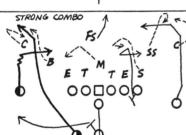

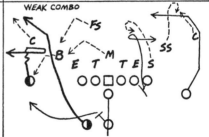

Diagram 3-11

Assignments

Split End: The split end is the outlet receiver. He runs a delay route.

Flankerback: The flankerback runs an in route. This moving route combines with the tight end's hook route to give the quarterback a good trouble outlet pattern.

47

Tight End: First, the tight end has pickup on the end man on the line of scrimmage. If the defender does not rush, he will run a hook route. This route combines with the flankerback's in route to give the quarterback a good trouble outlet pattern.

Fullback: The fullback has pickup on his assigned linebacker and then runs a trail route. He will provide the quarterback with a good trouble outlet.

Halfback: The halfback is the primary receiver. He does not have pickup. On the snap he runs a 17-yard fan route.

Quarterback: The quarterback takes a seven-step drop and delivers his pass to his primary receiver—the halfback running the fan route. Should the throwing lane to the halfback be threatened, he will option his pass to his outlet receiver—the split end running the delay route.

59 QUICK OUT-STOP (DIAGRAM 3-12)

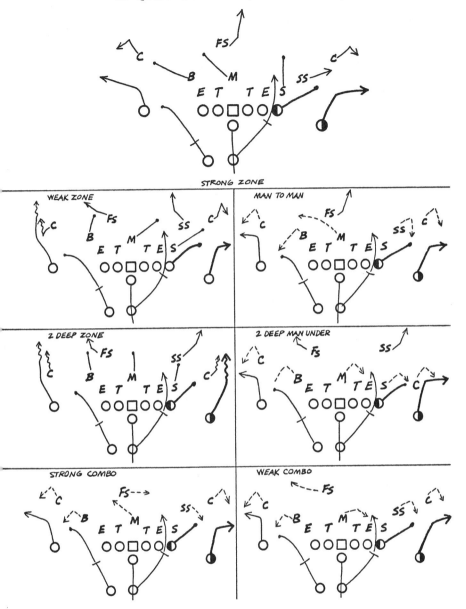

Diagram 3-12

Assignments

Split End and Flankerback: The receiver runs a quick out route. On 59 Quick Out-Stop the flankerback is the primary receiver, and on 58 Quick Out-Stop the split end becomes the primary receiver.

Tight End: On 59 Quick Out-Stop, the tight end is the outlet receiver. He runs a 2-yard stop route.

Fullback: The fullback has pickup on his assigned linebacker and then runs a close route to hold inside undercover defenders to their areas of responsibility.

Halfback: The halfback has pickup on his assigned linebacker and then runs a 2-yard route. On 58 Quick Out-Stop, he becomes the outlet receiver.

Quarterback: The quarterback takes a three-step drop and delivers his pass to his primary receiver—the flankerback running the quick out route. Should the throwing lane to the flankerback be threatened, he will option his pass to his outlet receiver—the tight end running the 2-yard stop route.

59 SLANT WIDE (DIAGRAM 3-13)

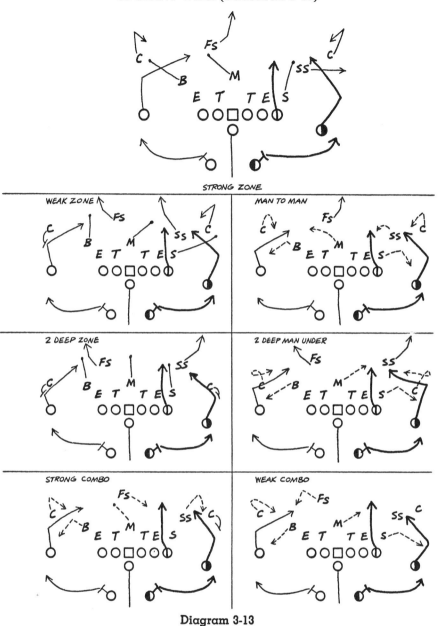

Diagram 3-13

Assignments

Split End and Flankerback: The receiver runs a slant route. On 59 Slant Wide the flankerback is the primary receiver, and on 58 Slant Wide the split end becomes the primary receiver.

Tight End: The tight end runs a hook route to hold inside undercover defenders to their areas of responsibility. He must always be alert for a quick pass, should a particular dog or coverage leave him open.

Fullback and Halfback: The back has pickup on his assigned linebacker and then runs a wide route. On 59 Slant Wide the fullback is the outlet receiver, and on 58 Slant Wide the halfback becomes the outlet receiver.

Quarterback: The quarterback takes a three-step drop and delivers his pass to his primary receiver—the flankerback running the slant route. Should the throwing lane to the flankerback be threatened, he will option his pass to his outlet receiver—the fullback running the wide route.

These pattern designs with Air Option principles are devastating against any defensive coverage. They represent the base to exploit any defensive scheme. Develop a precision passer, protect the passer, train the skilled receivers and backs to explode into their routes, and enjoy the rewards. It is a fascinating picture to view.

Chapter 4

QUARTERBACK

AIR OPTION TECHNIQUES

THE timing and consistency of the quarterback's pass is a most vital part of the Air Option. His dropback and delivery time must be exact. His seven-step dropback should take him 10 yards off the line of scrimmage in 1.8 seconds. From the snap, he should be able to set up and release the football in 2.8 seconds.

These standards are demanding and can only be met by utilizing the proper technique. It all begins with the stance.

STANCE

The quarterback's stance is very important to the entire setting action. His feet should be flat on the turf, directly below his armpits and pointing straight ahead. His weight is pressed forward to the balls of the feet and toes, but mentally he is prepared to push off his left foot. This weight distribution will allow him to snap away from the center on his dropback without taking a false step to adjust his body weight. Very few quarterbacks practice this important point. By false-stepping most put themselves behind schedule right from the beginning. The knees and ankles are comfortably flexed, and the hips are slightly closed to draw the knees in line with the big toes. This places the quarterback in the best position to quickly push off and begin his dropback.

With a wrist-deep position and fingers spread, he sets the middle finger of his right hand on the crease of the center's rear. The left hand is spread and points down the center's left leg. The thumbs are held together, with the first joint of the bottom thumb placed in the groove between the first and second joint of the top thumb. This will place his hands in the best position to grasp the meat of the football. The hands cannot be separated during the snap.

The quarterback should keep a firm press on the center's rear and enough bend in the elbows to keep this press by extending the arms during the snap. The quick-drop step utilized in his dropback technique tends to pull him away from the center; therefore, this technique becomes particularly important.

CENTER-QUARTERBACK EXCHANGE

The center's right hand and arm drive the football back as quickly, solidly, and accurately as possible to the quarterback's hands. The snapper's right hand will rotate palm up during the snap. He lifts the football, bending his elbow slightly and turning the wrist naturally to place the ball in the quarterback's hands. The laces should hit along the first joints of the passer's fingers where only a slight tilt of the ball is needed for the proper throwing grip.

To test the accuracy of the snap, the quarterback need only drop his bottom hand and let the center snap to his top hand. The adjustment for a poor snap can easily be seen from the direction the football bounces off the quarterback's top hand. If the ball hits properly it will nearly stick to the quarterback's hand and then drop straight down to the turf. If the quarterback pulls his hands out too early, the ball will bounce off the center's rear up into the air.

SPRINTBACK TECHNIQUE

The sprintback is the dropback technique used by the Air Option quarterback to move to his launch point. The speed and depth of the dropback required by the Air Option makes it necessary to use this technique. With the sprintback technique most quarterbacks can learn to drop back and set up at a depth of 10 yards in 1.8 seconds. Because of the speed with which he can set up and deliver the ball, the sprintback quarterback is more easily protected. Also, the speed of the sprintback is consistent and times precisely with Air Option patterns.

SPRINTBACK SEQUENCE

On the snap count, the quarterback sets back slightly to shift his body weight in the direction of his drop. At the same time, he will begin to step with his right foot, transferring all of his weight to his left. Because he controls the cadence, the quarterback can time this quick-drop step so that he is taking it while the snap is coming back. This will give him a head start. It is very important that this drop step be simultaneous with the count. Alert defensive linemen learn to key even the slightest movement by the quarterback before the snap.

The quarterback must keep a solid press and ride the center with his hands to receive the exchange. As the football hits his hands, he will already be rolling off his left foot and shifting his weight to his right. As the weight changes to his right foot, his left crosses over for the second step (Diagram 4-1). During these two steps, his hips should turn nearly to the opposite goal line—almost 180 degrees. This hip position will allow him to spring to his launch point with full, smooth strides. Many quarterbacks limit their stride and slow their dropback by turning only 90 degrees (Diagram 4-2).

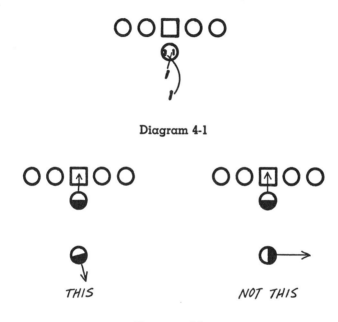

Diagram 4-1

Diagram 4-2

The quarterback's head and shoulders are turned so that his eyes can remain downfield. He must be able to see the entire pass defense coverage. A quarterback's vision and ability to attack pass coverage can improve tremendously. This skill is a major topic that will be covered later in this chapter. The first prerequisite to developing this skill is to focus the eyes on the coverage.

The quick-drop step during the snap and the crossover stride combine with the snap count to get the quarterback from two to three yards deep before a defender can even cross the scrimmage line. From here the quarterback will sprint back to his launch point with maximum controlled speed. His arms move in a normal running action while securing the football. The ball is carried comfortably just below the numbers and flows back and forth across his body to permit the arms to move.

The run should be smoother, and there should be harmony between the rate and length of stride. Initially, the quarterback will have to make a conscious effort to lengthen his stride in order to get his full 10 yards depth in seven strides. Once the proper stride length is grooved, it will require only occasional attention.

The quarterback continues to accelerate through the fourth stride of his sprintback. On his fifth stride, he should hit flat-footed and come under control in preparation for his setup. He actually begins to shift his weight, and his body line is almost straight up and down at this point. By his sixth step, his body weight is slightly forward to allow him to hit this step explosively enough to stop nearly all of his backward motion. His seventh step is planted with his right foot flat on the turf as he comes to a complete stop in the set position.

Planting the right foot flat on the turf will provide the base to begin the passing motion. With the proper setup, he will have enough body control to pass from this set position without having to shuffle forward to greater control. The foot should be set perpendicular with a line between him and his primary receiver. This will cause his left hip to be in line with the passing target (Diagram 4-3).

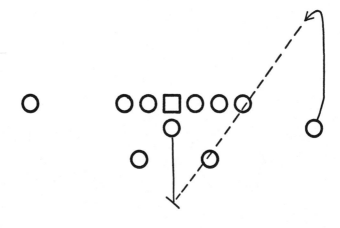

Diagram 4-3

By placing the hips and upper body in this position, the passer can uncoil to whip a timed pass to this primary receiver. If the throwing lane to the primary is clear, the setup actually flows right into the passing motion. As the passer sets, he rocks back to stand tall in the set position and then immediately rocks forward again to deliver the football. The set and throw is a continuous motion. His seventh step hits the turf in 1.8 seconds and flows right into a release in 2.8 seconds.

If the throwing lane to his primary is threatened, the quarterback bounces to the balls of his feet as he looks to his outlet receiver. This will naturally adjust his hip and shoulder direction so that he can deliver the ball to his new target. The release time to his outlet receiver will be 3.0 to 3.2 seconds.

The basic Air Option passing game is built around the seven-step drop. However, the three-step drop will be utilized for the quick game and the five-step drop for some of the play action and screens. Many top passing coaches have been successful with the five-step drop involving the medium range pass for their basic attack. The five-step drop requires a hitch step forward after bouncing on the fifth step. The passes must be timed expertly and not allow the receiver to utilize his bag of techniques in running various routes. He must cut sharply and be on time. In a study of quarterback "sacks," the five-step drop leads the seven-step drop almost double. Common sense speaks out to indicate the deeper the quarterback sprints from the line of scrimmage (seven steps), the better his opportunity to remain in a standing position. However, it is important to teach the five-step drop for certain patterns.

THROWING MOTION

The quarterback's throwing motion must be natural and uniquely his own style. He has developed this style over a period of years, and any attempt to alter this technique should be very slight and done only after careful study. Therefore, the following is just a guide and must be adapted to the individual quarterback.

In the set position, the quarterback has a slight flex in his knees and hips. It is the explosive extension of his right knee and hip that starts the body rotation or uncoiling and generates most of the power of the pass.

The quarterback's weight will shift from his right foot to his left as he snaps his hips—which an instant later pulls the shoulders around to whip his passing arm forward. A short guide step just to the left of the throwing line will allow the passer the necessary hip rotation. If this guide step were on or to the right of the throwing line, the hip rotation would be blocked by the lead leg.

The passer should land with his weight on the ball of his guide-step foot and have a slight flex in that knee. This will prevent overstriding. When a passer overstrides, he will land heel-first on a straight leg. This is a most prevalent technique flaw and will limit a passer's body rotation and consequently the velocity of his pass.

The left arm should aid the rotation of the upper body. The left arm is slightly flexed and about shoulder high as the left shoulder pulls down and back to whip the right shoulder and passing arm through high overhead.

The passing arm carries the ball down and around the shoulder joint and then up in a forward arc toward the release. The quarterback's delivery should be high and away from his head where he can feel the sensation of having his power on top of the ball, whipping it forward. The arm action is not a strained, overhead motion. It is a three-fourths overhead delivery—but because of the shoulder tilt, the ball passes nearly straight above the center of gravity. As the ball is released, the wrist turns down and out so that the outside of the index finger is the last part of the hand to leave the ball. This wrist snap gives added zip to the ball and tightens the spiral.

The quarterback should grip the ball with the fingers and thumb spread comfortably. The little finger is about a half inch past the middle of the ball and just below the laces. The first joint of the ring finger is hooked over the laces just short of the middle of the ball. The other fingers are spread with the index finger placed no closer than an inch and a half to the back end of the ball. The thumb should be well-spread around the football about 2 inches from the back tip. The ball is tilted back slightly so there is space between it and the palm of the hand. It is gripped with firm, tacky pressure from the upper part of the fingers. A rigid grip takes away from the passer's touch and control of the ball. The correct grip will allow him to throw flat, medium, and high arc passes without adjusting his hand position.

OPTION PASSING

Air Option patterns are designed to put two receivers on one pass defender. The quarterback simply options to the uncovered receiver. In the example below, the weakside linebacker has been isolated and forced to defend against both the tight end and the halfback.

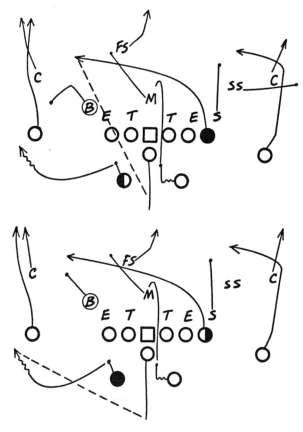

Diagram 4-4

The quarterback is given a primary receiver (in this case the tight end) to whom he will deliver a pass. If a defender is in a position to threaten that passing lane, the quarterback will set up and drop the ball off to an outlet receiver—in this case, the halfback on a wide flare route (Diagram 4-4).

VISION AND CONCENTRATION

With the many pass coverages the quarterback will be passing against, it is important that he not anticipate keying a particular defender. The coverage is insignificant from a cognitive standpoint. The passer will option any defender who attempts to cover a pass defense zone.

The option must be a reaction. This reaction will be developed only if the quarterback makes repeated pass attempts into the coverage affecting the pattern and applies the proper concentration principles.

He should direct his concentration to his primary receiver, see the coverage with soft focus, and let his subconscious mind sort out the coverage. From here he will learn to react spontaneously with a pass to the open receiver. By directing his concentration onto his primary receiver, he will insure true reaction passing, turning the passing decision to his subconscious mind. Reaction passing is not complicated by trying to decide what a pass defender will do or wondering, "What now, Coach; they are dropping nine pass defenders?"

The quarterback will also need his eyes to fine-tune his accuracy. As he begins his delivery, he should switch from a soft focus on the coverage to a fine focus on his receiver.

By concentrating on a small target, such as the receiver's chin strap, the passer will have a concentration point on which he can zero-in his fine focus. He cannot force this concentration or attempt to aim the ball at this point. Rather, he should direct his attention to the concentration point and let his mind focus itself.

The quarterback must also develop an interest in this concentration point for it to hold his attention. Mentally measuring the distance the ball misses the point serves the purpose. This technique will also give the quarterback accurate feedback on his pass—an absolute necessity for improving accuracy.

By focusing on a concentration point, the quarterback's conscious mind will be totally absorbed and unable to interfere with the delivery. The result will be a smooth, spontaneous delivery of astonishing accuracy.

FOLLOW-THROUGH

The "follow-through" phase is the physical continuation of vision and concentration.

Once the passer releases the pass toward the concentration point, he must keep his eyes on the target, keep his passing hand pointed toward the target, and step toward it with his back foot. This will keep the ball on target and prevent the passer from short-changing the delivery. A bad habit for a passer is stepping back after the release. This not only takes the power out of the pass, but oftentimes the ball goes sailing over the head of the intended receiver.

Another important reason for the follow-through is to keep the quarterback "in the game." Should a defender step in front of the receiver and pick off the pass for an interception, the quarterback must alert his team by calling the direction of the interception—right - left - middle—to gather his teammates to the scene of action to prevent a long run back. This is not a negative response, but part of the game—a sudden switch to defense.

Another vital reason for the follow-through is the "safety" clause. The rusher is bearing down on the passer, when the quarterback steps back he becomes a bigger target. Moving up into the pocket keeps the quarterback in a better position to absorb the "blow" should it come.

The "eyes" in football are instrumental to the scientific approach in accomplishing the highest award. The eyes are used in every facet of the game. The blocker looks at the point to be blocked. The quarterback looks the ball into the running back's stomach for the handoff. In other sports, the baseball hitter must see the ball; the golfer picks out a small area of the ball to hit to perfect his swing. The eyes are the concentration of accomplishment.

The important fact to understand, however, is that the eyes begin every action. Many coaches teach in reverse. For example, the coach teaches the quarterback to take certain steps on a handoff to the running back and then look the ball into the pocket. He should teach him to look toward the running back's pocket (belt buckle) first, then the steps will follow. This is natural because our muscular reactions follow what we see in a natural sense. The offensive line coach teaches the pulling guard to swing his arms, pivot, move down the line, and pick out his block. He should teach him to pick out the defender with his eyes first, and then he will naturally swing his arms, pivot, and drive toward the point.

I learned this concept from one of the greatest teachers in the game, Blanton Collier, former Head Coach of the World-Champion Cleveland Browns. My association with Blanton in the early years took me to the Cleveland Browns' camp where I met Paul Brown, the most successful Head Coach in the profession. Several years later, this association provided me the opportunity to become the Head Coach of the Cincinnati Bengals.

In 1976, I introduced Steve Moore to Blanton Collier. Steve's exposure to this great man aided his development and comprehension of the correct teaching methods.

The majority of the top coaches in the NFL past and present are disciples of Blanton Collier and Paul Brown. My early association with both Paul Brown and Blanton Collier shaped my coaching career and influenced me to become highly organized and teach technical football in detail.

Chapter 5

QUARTERBACK

DEVELOPMENT

T HE Air Option demands a lot of the quarterback. It is a precisioned passing game, and his dropback, his option, his reaction, the timing of his delivery, and his touch on the ball are of tremendous importance to its execution. As the quarterback improves his skills, he will be able to direct the Air Option attack and generate many points.

The quarterback's developmental program is divided into two phases: in-season and off-season.

IN-SEASON PASSING SEQUENCE

The in-season passing sequence combines drills for the quarterback to improve his perception of the coverage, his option reaction, and his timing with his receivers. The following passing drills are integrated into the workout schedule.

Passing Warmup

Two passers should begin 10 yards apart. Each warmup throw should start with the setup (move only one step) and go through the perfect throwing action. After each pass, they should take one step backwards until they are 20 yards apart. At this point, they continue to pass until each "feels" his throwing arm is completely ready. At the beginning of the drill, they just ease the ball to each other and then build to where they really zip it back and forth.

Should receivers be available, a receiver should be assigned to a quarterback to receive the passes thrown to him. The receiver should start his concentration of looking the ball in, putting it under his arm, and then handing the football to the quarterback. This beginning drill allows the receivers to experience the "feel" of the ball.

During the drill the quarterback also begins warming up his concentration. He should pick out a concentration point and let his throwing flow to that point.

Long Arc Drill (Diagram 5-1)

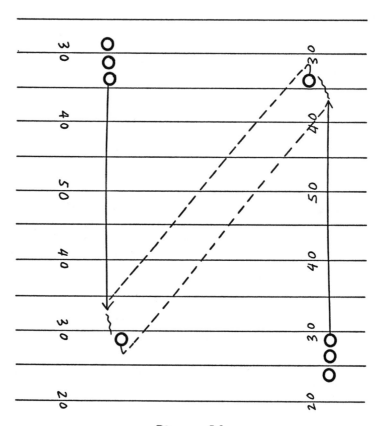

Diagram 5-1

The quarterback takes one step back to set up and delivers the ball to the receiver striding downfield. He begins passing short and then lengthens his passes just short of his maximum distance. He should vary his passes throughout the trajectory range. He must develop the "feel" of stretching the receiver downfield. Also, he learns another important technique—the "spin" of the ball. The ball always spins outward; therefore, as the distance increases, the ball travels higher and accelerates the spin process. This means the target must be adjusted to offset the spinning (Diagram 5-2).

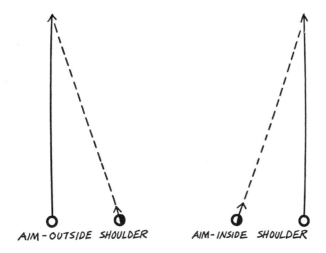

AIM - OUTSIDE SHOULDER   AIM - INSIDE SHOULDER

Diagram 5-2

Hook-Up Drill (10 Minutes)

In this drill, the quarterback fine-tunes his timing and accuracy to his receiver's step routes. Here he will simply take the snap, move to his launch point, and deliver the ball to his receiver. It is important that he pass equally to both his right and left. This is the drill where the coach checks the quarterback's mechanics and the timing of his drop and release (Diagram 5-3).

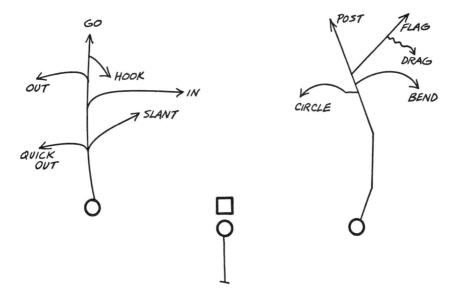

Diagram 5-3

Reaction Drill (10 Minutes)

Pass plays are broken down to the quarterback and his primary receiver and a stationary outlet receiver. The defender positioned to stop this segment of the pass play moves to defend the play, simulating the play of the next opponent. Through repetition the quarterback will learn the correct reactions to these defenses. The key coaching point is for the quarterback to lock onto the concentration point of his primary receiver, letting the subconscious mind sort out the defensive picture, and then react to his outlet receiver if his throwing lane to his primary is threatened (Diagram 5-4).

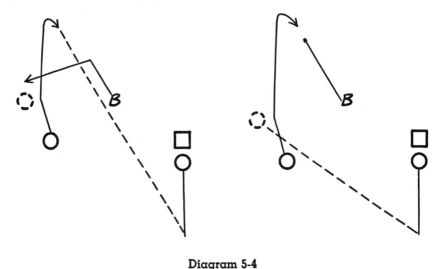

Diagram 5-4

Skeleton Passing Drill (20 Minutes)

The skeleton passing drill is designed to give the full passing complement (quarterback, backs, and receivers) an opportunity to coordinate the pass offense to the opponent's coverages. The goal is to give the quarterbacks and receivers a maximum number of quality repetitions in order to bring each pass play to a high level of proficiency as rapidly as possible.

Setup: The starting defensive backs and linebackers provide the pass defense. The alignment and movement of this unit must be accurate and give the picture of the next opponent. Three or four reserve players fill the down line positions and complete the defensive picture. The defensive line will cross the line of scrimmage 2 to 3 yards to create the distraction of a pass rush (Diagram 5-5). A center is joined by the kickers or reserve players who align in the offensive guard and tackle positions. Together with the defensive line, they will create the pass-block, pass-rush distraction.

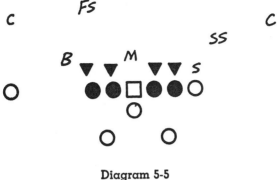

Diagram 5-5

The entire passing complement is in the drill: quarterback, split end, flanker, tight end, halfback, and fullback. The first two units alternate every other play. Starting quarterback will take three turns to the second teamer's one. Any third team players in the drill will alternate with the second team. The first unit should always stay intact.

The coach will call the pass plays from a script, with emphasis given to those that will be key plays that particular week, or those who are not up to par and need more drill.

The passing team will break the huddle and quickly move to the line of scrimmage. It is almost a race to see how fast the team can call a play and get the ball off.

After the play, backs and receivers will jog back until they are clear of the backs of the next group. Quarterbacks waiting their turns should throw passes to these players on their way back.

Additional Coaching Points

Attention is given to drill in all field positions, and down and distance situations.

Once every five or six plays one of the defensive linemen should rush the passer, forcing the quarterback to save the play by hitting a quick outlet or by throwing the ball away, or by escaping the rush and quickly scrambling back to the line of scrimmage.

Occasionally, the defensive coach will tell the defense the play so that the offense can learn to deal with a well-defended play. The quarterback will learn to hit an outlet receiver, or throw the ball away, or simply to save the play by scrambling back to the line of scrimmage.

Each quarterback's attempts, completions, percentage of completions, and interceptions should be recorded daily, as well as receivers' attempts, receptions. drops, and great catches.

Date _____

OB	Attempts	Completions	% Completed	Interceptions
1.				
2.				
3.				

Receivers	Attempts	Completions	%Completed	Interceptions
1.				
2.				
3.				
4.				

The in-season passing sequence must be accomplished before the formal practice session begins. This is a specialty period that adequately develops and masters the Air Option offensive attack. It is always an excellent teaching period and allows the skilled coaches to fine-tune the technical aspects of the passing parade.

QUARTERBACK OFF-SEASON PASSING SEQUENCE

In the off-season, the quarterback should work every other day or at least four days each week on his passing sequence. The sequence takes one hour to complete and is designed for him to develop his mechanics, passing strength, and accuracy.

The passing drills are done in sets of ten passes. The quarterback should have a bag of ten balls so that he can move quickly through each set without having to stop to chase footballs. A passing net that World Sporting Goods manufactures is also needed for the drills. This net has a red dot in its catching pocket that the quarterback can use as his concentration point.

Warmup

After warming up with striding and stretching exercises, the quarterback begins the passing sequence by warming up his passing arm. The passing warmup is done in the same manner as in the in-season passing sequence. It will take about 20 passes to efficiently warm up the throwing arm to where he can zip the ball 20 yards to the passing net.

Setup (10 Passes)

In this drill, the quarterback aligns in his normal stance, just in front of the passing net. On the quick count of his cadence, he sprints back seven steps, sets up, and passes the ball into the net. His concentration should be on the red dot in the center of the net, but he should also be aware of his sprintback and setup. He should work for a smooth, quick dropback that gets him the full 10 yards depth, free from any false steps. His setup should be sharp and balanced where it will lead right into a quick delivery. Both the setup and release time should be recorded once a week to chart the progress made.

Long Arc (16–22 Passes)

This drill helps the quarterback develop arm strength and the release necessary to throw the high arc for the long ball. To begin this drill, he aligns in his

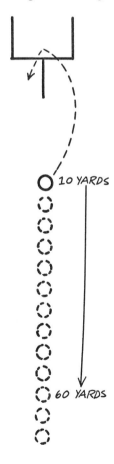

Diagram 5-6

normal stance 10 yards in front of the goal post. On his cadence he takes a three-step dropback, sets up, and delivers the ball just over the crossbar. By passing a high arc, the ball will drop close to the goal post on the other side (Diagram 5-6).

After two passes, he moves back 5 yards farther from the goal post and repeats the drill. The quarterback should continue to move back at 5-yard intervals until he can no longer reach the goal post with his pass.

Net Drill (150 Passes) (Diagram 5-7)

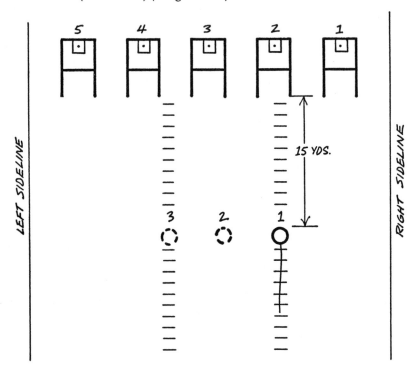

Diagram 5-7

The net is placed in position 1 to 2 yards from the sideline and 15 yards downfield from the quarterback's starting position. This is the approximate position where the wide receiver would catch the out route.

The quarterback begins the drill on the near hashmark. From this starting position, he will take his seven-step dropback and deliver the ball to the net. From the time he sets up until the ball strikes the target, his total concentration must be on the small red dot in the center of the net. It is this fine focus on the small target that is the key to developing pinpoint accuracy. He will throw ten passes from this hashmark before moving to the middle of the field for ten passes, and then to the far hashmark for ten more passes.

It is not necessary to take the full dropback for each pass. This is a passing drill, not a conditioning drill, and taking the full dropback every fifth pass is sufficient. The rest of the passes can be thrown after taking the last three steps of the dropback. The drill will be repeated with the net in each of the five positions for a total of 150 passes. These passes should be charted so that the quarterback can gauge his progress.

Date	Target 1	Target 2	Target 3	Target 4	Target 5	Total

This drill is very challenging, and in the beginning the number of hits will be low. However, if the quarterback continues to focus on the center of the target, his accuracy will make steady progress.

With the warmup passes, the quarterback will be throwing approximately 200 passes. If the drills are done properly, he will be working on the fundamental elements that need development in the off-season: technique, arm strength, and passing concentration.

The Program

The quarterback passing program involves a plan. To begin with, the quarterback coach should check the anatomy of each of his candidates. Height is important, but not totally necessary. The taller the quarterback, the better vision he should have—but some of our great quarterbacks have been around the 5'11" height. Some people believe if the quarterback is tall, he will be a better passer. The advantage of being tall helps only with vision. The length of the arm span in relation to the person's height does add greatly to the passer's potential. A long arm span will aid the individual in throwing a football over a shorter arm span. Also, a larger hand is an asset over the smaller hand because of the grip of the football. If the hand is large or has long fingers with flexibility, it will give the passer a distinct advantage. Fingers with flexibility will bend and stretch with the ball, enabling the passer to have complete control over the football. Stiff hands never help a passer. He invariably drops the ball and never seems to have control of his grip. A small hand that cannot completely grip the ball results in the passer pushing the ball.

One thing the quarterback coach must keep in mind: work as much individually (technique) with each candidate as possible. Group instructions have many pitfalls. Each passer will be different, and, therefore, he needs separate instructions and learning habits.

Before the coach begins instruction procedures on the grip-setting, and throwing action, he should observe the candidate's natural way of passing. It is dangerous to change a passer's grip or throwing action if the end result is productive. The coach may need only to adjust a part of the throwing action or the grip.

The training program starts first with the grip. The smaller the hand, the closer the fingers should move toward the end of the ball. The fingers should fit the ball firmly, but never too tightly. There should be air between the palm of the hand and the ball. The fingers actually control the ball.

After developing a firm grip to control the ball, the quarterback next learns a setting action before he begins his throwing action. This requires getting away from the center quickly. The seven-step drop is most important. Seven steps for most quarterbacks will put him 9½ to 10 yards deep. This depth greatly aids the quarterback and the protectors. It allows the quarterback to see his receivers better and start his throwing action when he sets up. Five steps are used primarily with intermediate timing patterns; three steps for short, quick passes. The seven-steps setting action coordinates with the step-counting of the receivers for the deeper timing factor.

The setting action starts with the quarterback moving away from the center. Failure to move away from the center swiftly is critical for the entire passing game. Most passing plans bog down at this stage if the correct technique is not applied. It all begins with the quarterback's stance, cadence, and first step.

The toes must be digging into the ground to anchor the quarterback to eliminate false steps when he starts to pull out from the center. If the quarterback has his weight on his heels, he will take at least two false steps before he actually begins a backward sprint. This not only hinders the quarterback in setting up at seven steps, but also will cost the offensive team valuable time and destroy the timing aspect of the patterns. On the cadence call to snap the ball, the quarterback must first drop his right foot back, keeping the weight on his left foot and keeping his hands under the center for the snap. It must be remembered, the cadence is a true reaction sound. The center will snap the ball upon hearing the sound. Therefore, should the quarterback pull out on his sound, he will pull away from the ball and be ahead of the team. The quarterback must remain under the center, pressing weight on his left foot, keeping his eyes straight ahead, and moving his right foot out. As the ball hits his hands, he must then push off the left foot, transferring the weight to the right foot. As the weight transfers to the right foot, the left leg crosses over for the second step. From that point on it becomes a sprintback, completing seven steps and the setting motion, to prepare for the throwing action. As the quarterback moves away from the center, he must turn his hips toward the opponent's goalline and sprint back the required seven steps. As he is sprinting back, he must keep his head turned downfield toward his own goalline, looking over his left shoulder as he retreats. This allows him to see his "reads" and the linebackers blitzing. Not enough can be said with regard to quickness in setting up properly. Unless this is accomplished, the quarterback can never be an above-average passer. The drop-step crossover method will enable the quarterback to gain a depth of 3 yards from the center before a defender can cross the line of scrimmage. The continuance of seven steps allows the quarterback to set up comfortably and start his throwing action before the rusher can get within 3 yards of the passer. This aids the passer's vision and gives him the confidence to drill the football through the passing lanes.

The setting action should be timed to indicate progress. The quarterback should work to set up at seven steps in 1.8 seconds. As he sets up, his throwing action should begin with the ball leaving his hand in 2.8 seconds or less. Greg Cook, Tommy Kramer, and others worked very hard on their own during the summer months. They learned to set at 10 yards in 1.7 seconds and have the pass away in 2.7 seconds. It takes hard work to accomplish this feat, and they were willing to pay the price to succeed. I believe this one single thing makes the difference between a quarterback becoming an average or above-average passer. As it turned out, many advanced to the "great" category.

The throwing action is the next area to observe and constructively adjust. Again, it is important to observe the natural way the passer delivers the forward pass. This may indicate that he does not need any additional instruction or only slight adjustment. The throwing action should actually begin as the quarterback hits on his seventh step which will end up on his right foot. This step is the stopping point. The seventh step serves as a brake to stop, stand tall with feet comfortably spread, and with the ball in both hands about chest high. At this point, the passer should begin his throwing action providing the primary receiver's path has indicated the pass is ready to be delivered.

As the quarterback sets, his body will actually be parallel to the sideline. As the arm is being raised for the pass, the end of the ball points toward the sideline before the ball is brought back over the ear and higher than the headgear. Once the throwing action starts forward, the forward point of the ball rotates toward the receiver. As the wrist snaps downward and outward, the ball is released with the back of the hand visible and the palm pointing outward. This keeps the point of the ball up and easy to catch. If the palm of the hand shows, the ball has a hard downward movement. It has the same effect as a pitcher throwing a curve or hook—it is very difficult to catch. More importantly, this movement of the elbow and wrist will not get the full, smooth benefit of the perfect pass as with the palm-out method.

The delivery is actually a transfer of weight from the back (right) foot to the front (left) foot. The transferring of weight produces the follow-through necessary to drive the football on target with the necessary force. As the weight is being brought forward, it is important for the passer to point his foot (left) toward the target preventing himself from throwing across his body. This passing technique executes a smooth, relaxed throwing action that is totally necessary in the development of the quarterback.

The left hand coming off the ball as the quarterback cocks the ball in his right hand serves as a balancing measure. Some quarterbacks point with the left arm, some swing it aside as the ball is released—but whichever method is used, it should have a natural "feel" to balance the body for the release.

The guide step with the front foot and the rolling of the hips may be the most important phase of the passing action. I have always believed the stride should be a short step. This forces the hips to turn stronger and compels the passer to follow through by taking an additional step with his right foot. It must be understood that the power of the throwing action is mostly in the hips. A long stride extends the passer to a point where he loses the all-important power because he is throwing with only his arm, and the weight remains mostly on the back foot. If the reader will study the great golfer, shot-putter, baseball hitter, and passer, one will understand my theory. The hips generate the power. One common fault of most is the problem of dropping the ball down to the hip as part of the throwing motion. This forces a full windup, losing time. Also, it tends to prevent the passer from shifting the weight to the forward foot. To correct this, have the quarterback move his right foot first in the shuffle forward as he begins the passing action. This prevents the dropping of the ball. Correct the feet movement, and you will correct the throwing motion.

Once the quarterback develops a smooth, relaxed, confident throwing action, it is time to move on to discuss concentration. Instructions on concentration should never be mentioned until after the quarterback has the mechanics of the center-quarterback exchange, setting up, and throwing action conquered. He must be able to execute the mechanical phase in his subsconscious mind, whereby he does not have to concentrate on what he is attempting to master. It must be repeated so often that it becomes automatic and habit-forming. Repetition is the only answer, provided it is done correctly. If the quarterback repeats this portion of his mechanics incorrectly, he is then going in reverse. Here lies the importance of proper instruction. The instructor is not correct in continuing to have the quarterback repeat the wrong procedure. It would be best to let the player work it out on his own in his natural way. I think this is what Bud Wilkinson, the famed Oklahoma coach, meant when he referred to "overcoaching" the player to the point where he loses all his initiative and aggressiveness. The best coach is not always the one who jumps around yelling instructions. Enthusiasm is most important as long as the instruction is constructive.

As the quarterback is going back into the pocket to set up, he is recognizing the defensive "reads" that will give him the reaction to which receiver will be his primary target. This must be a reaction and not a concentration, because the full concentration of the quarterback's mind must be on the target. He must "zero in" on the receiver and pinpoint his passes. For example, the receiver has turned into a hook pattern. The quarterback must pick out a small object on the receiver for his concentration spot and drill the football toward that small object. All quarterbacks are different in what they select visibly as a concentration point.

Rick Norton, while at Kentucky, picked out the lips or the teeth of the receivers. Others use a number on the jersey, or the area between the numbers. The theory behind this concentration area is simple. The smaller the target, the closer the pass will end up around the target. Should the quarterback concentrate on the whole receiver, he will throw somewhere around the whole target. This theory will produce pinpoint passing if completely understood.

The circle (hook) type pass is easier because the quarterback can pick out an object on the receiver. When throwing the bend-type (sideline) route, it becomes more difficult because the quarterback is throwing toward air. He must pick out an imaginary object such as the belt buckle and drill the pass toward that small area. This method is also very successful.

Concentration is blotting out everything else but the small object at that moment, and then going through the perfect, smooth, relaxed throwing action that occurs in the subconscious mind. Learning and carrying out this theory is the difference between being an average or great passer.

It must be pointed out to the passer that he never really aims toward the target. His eyes locate the target with full concentration; then the body reacts into the throwing action. Once the passer presses himself and attempts to aim the ball, he might as well go back to the first grade and start again.

As time goes on, the quarterback learns the tricks of the trade, such as the use of the eyes and head to take a defender off of the receiver for a split second before he drills the ball. This is called "looking the defender off." It can be very effective on linebackers and a middle safety. Also, the pumping of the ball or faking the ball can be effective. These are "extras" that come later as the passer gains experience. Another trick is learning to throw the ball away when the receiver is covered and not take the big loss. Greg Cook became so good at this that it contributed directly to his winning the national total offensive yardage in 1968. Most passers take a lot of losses because they end up "eating the football" when the receiver is covered. Greg mastered the trait of "getting rid of the ball" and preventing the loss of yardage. This kept him from having minus yards in the rushing department. Along with his "keep" gains in the triple and his passing completion yards, he was able to amass 3,272 yards for one season—the best mark in the U.S.A. All of the "little extras" come with time and experience.

In 1963 at the NCAA Convention in Chicago, I sat in a hotel room and listened intently to John Bridgers of Baylor University. Coach Bridgers was one of the country's most successful passing coaches. I shall never forget his expression, "the quarterback should feel a sense of belonging to the ball." He went on to explain some drills he used to train his great quarterbacks at Baylor. I incorporated some of his drills into my training program because of my high respect and regard for his mastery of the passing game.

The sense of belonging to the ball was incorporated into the fancy drill. The fancy drill involves: dropping the ball and catching it with the same hand, switching hands, swinging the ball from the hand around the back and rotating under each leg. I can assure the reader when this drill is accomplished, the ball appears to be glued to the quarterback's fingers. This is a good drill for the passer to perform before he begins practice.

Another drill that should be incorporated into some phase of the teaching

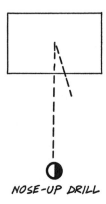

NOSE-UP DRILL

Diagram 5-8

process is the ''nose-up'' drill (Diagram 5-8). This is to teach the passer two things: the strength of the wrist-snap for the forward pass, and the art of keeping the nose of the ball up so it will carry in flight and be easily caught by the receiver. The passer should stand 7 or 8 yards away from a board or some hard surface (10 feet in height). He must stand flatfooted, facing the board with the passing arm high over his head. The ball is snapped from that position, allowing only the wrist to direct the ball to the board.

When the ball bounces straight back or to the right of the passer, then the forward point of the ball is up, whereby the receiver can handle the pass easily. If the ball bounces back to the left of the passer, then the forward point is down. The passer can easily correct this by checking the ball as it is released from his hand. The palm of the hand must be turned toward the ground and slightly outward.

This drill will also strengthen the all-important wrist-snap. Rick Norton of Kentucky developed such a strong wrist-snap, he could literally flick the ball on a line up to 15 yards. Many times a quarterback will have rushers hanging on his legs, hips, and left shoulder, but if he can get the right arm up, he just might be able to wrist-snap the ball out to a flaring halfback for eventually a big gain.

Another useful drill is the hip drill (Diagram 5-9). The hip drill consists of checking the guide step, hip rotation, and follow-through. Realizing it can only be accomplished with the short step, the passer stands 10 yards wide and 5 yards deep from each side of the net. He passes ten times from the right side and ten times from the left side. In this drill, the passer is cognizant of his lead step, utilizing the power from the hips and driving the ball into the net with the correct follow-through.

Developing the quarterback is an ongoing task. Like the unfinished symphony, the training goes on and on. Throughout this book, the technique of the setting action, throwing motion, sorting out of the coverages, ''zeroing in'' on

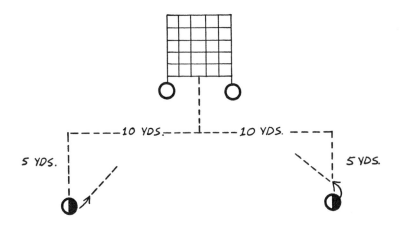

Diagram 5-9

the primary target, adjusting to the outlet receiver, drills, and various plans will be repeated over and over again. Correct repetition pays handsome dividends. The authors of this book have intentionally prepared *The Air Option Passing Game* in this manner to impress upon the readers its importance.

Chapter 6

RECEIVER TECHNIQUES

FOR THE AIR OPTION

SPEED, precision in route running, and consistency in catching the ball are the key ingredients to successful receiver play.

A receiver must have the speed to threaten deep. Without this deep threat, secondary defenders can crowd medium routes and destroy the entire design of the Air Option.

Precision in route running is critical. For the quarterback to develop precise timing and accuracy, the receiver must present him with routes that break at the right depth with the correct timing.

A successful receiver must also consistently catch every ball that touches his hands. The difference between winning and losing is often so small that making just one difficult catch could make that difference.

Proper technique will allow a receiver to achieve his speed, potential precision in his route running, and consistency in catching.

WIDE RECEIVER STANCE

A wide receiver should align in the proper stance to start explosively off the line of scrimmage. His stance should also put him in a good position to escape from holdup or funneling defenders. The three-point sprinter's stance meets both of these standards.

In the three-point sprinter's stance, the wide receiver will have his weight rolled forward where a forceful extension of his drive leg and hip will shoot him off the line with good body lean. He will not need to roll his body weight forward to initiate his forward momentum as is common with either the balanced three-point stance or the two-point up-stance. Also, because of the body lean and quick start that is realized from this starting position, the receiver can attack a holdup defender with the necessary upfield power to escape quickly from the defender.

In the three-point sprinter's stance, the receiver narrows his base by positioning his feet as a sprinter would in his starting blocks. His outside foot is dropped back where he can feel balanced. For consistency of step count patterns, the outside foot should always drop back.

The knees and hips are well flexed, poised for the explosive start, the outside hand is placed directly below the corresponding shoulder. The shoulders should be level to the ground and parallel to the line of scrimmage. The inside arm is flexed in the running position and with the wrist braced on the outside of the knee.

The head is up so that he can see the coverage as well as the ball which he will key for his start.

TIGHT END AND RUNNING BACK STANCE

The tight end and both running backs should be able to start explosively in a variety of directions. The tight end will need to release both inside or outside on his pass route or towards his blocking assignment, and the running back will have to move to carry out his assignment as a blocker, faker, ball carrier, or pass receiver.

A tight end or running back should use a three-point stance with little weight on the down hand. The feet should be spread about shoulder width apart. The preferred foot can be dropped back so that the toes are even with the instep of the front foot. The ankles are well flexed, and the feet remain flat on the turf. The weight is on the balls of the feet, and the toes claw the turf. This balance position and the clawing of the turf with the toes should prevent any false stepping or any other wasted motion on the start.

The knees are comfortably flexed, and the hips are tucked to keep the weight back on the balls of the feet. The down arm is straight down from the shoulder and is only used to help balance the body weight—not to support it. The other arm is flexed in the running position and braced with the wrist just above the knee. The shoulders are level to the ground and parallel to the line of scrimmage.

RELEASING FROM A TIGHT DEFENDER

When the receiver's release is threatened by a tight defender, he must use a technique that will insure a quick release off the line of scrimmage. Whether it be the tight end or a wide receiver, there are two essential ingredients in avoiding a delay. First, the receiver must stay low enough to prevent the defender from standing him up. If he were to lose his body lean, he would no longer have the leverage to explode upfield. He would immediately be thrown behind schedule for the timing of the route. From his stance the receiver must shoot by the defender on a low plane. He should stay on this low plane until he has reached a hip-to-toe relationship on the defender. Once this relationship is realized, the defender no longer may use his hands in his holdup of the receiver. The second essential is that the direction of the release must be upfield. If the receiver moves laterally to avoid the defender, his power will be funneled down the line of scrimmage, and his downfield speed and depth will be lost (Diagram 6-1).

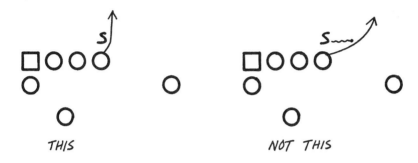

Diagram 6-1

Shoot-Out Release

This release can be used from a tight or wide alignment. From a good stance, the receiver shoots through the forcing unit or by the defender on a low plane but without going to his hands. Tremendous explosion must come from a complete and forceful extension of the drive hip and leg. By releasing tight to the defender with a strong upfield drive, the receiver will prevent the defender from funneling him down the line of scrimmage. He will rip his arm by the defender. A glancing blow off the defender will free the receiver. A short jab step or head fake in the opposite direction of the intended release can be added to this release as a change-up. However, the forward explosion is essential while the lateral jab step or head fake is secondary.

Arm-Over Release

The arm-over release is very similar to the defensive lineman's pass rush, commonly known as the swim or windmill technique. For an arm-over release to the right side, the receiver steps with his right foot directly at the defender's left shoulder. At the same time he clubs and grabs that shoulder with his right hand and pulls the defender, attempting to turn him and pull himself by the defender. As he pulls, he begins to move his left foot by the defender. As he continues his stride, he will "swim" his left hand over to the defender's back. A raking action with this arm may be necessary to pull the receiver by the defender.

SEPARATION TECHNIQUES

Separation techniques are used by the receiver to break free from the defender. Ninety-five percent of the time the only separation technique that a receiver will need is his route cut. There are times, however, that a defender is in a good position to stop a route, and the receiver is forced to maneuver or fake him just a little more. Variations and combinations of the following are limitless. A receiver needs only experiment to come up with his most effective way to separate from pass defenders.

Weave

The weave is a snakelike move where the receiver will break approximately 30 degrees every three steps. The move is accomplished with a shift in body weight and a smooth, easy cut. The weave will separate the receiver laterally from the defender.

Phony Acceleration

From a controlled run, the receiver can noticeably change his running action without affecting his forward speed a great deal. These changes in body lean and arm/leg action can be used to set up a short route cut. From the controlled run, the receiver tells the defender of his deep intentions by increasing the vigor of his arm and leg action. He will appear to have started a sprint deep. When the defender shifts his body weight back or pivots to gain depth, the receiver makes his short pattern cut.

Change of Pace

This fake is the reverse of the phony acceleration fake and is used to separate from a defender to run a deep route. The receiver will pause or push in the clutch to disengage the running action. This invites the defender to close on the receiver. As the defender closes, the receiver regains his acceleration.

Stutter

This fake is used to set up deep patterns and uses the same principle of drawing the defender as the change of pace. From a controlled run he will throw his head and shoulders back, leaning back as if to initiate a pattern cut. This action is much more abrupt than a change of pace. This standup action and the foot stutter are simultaneous and last just for an instant. As the defender reacts, the receiver will have already continued deep. This is a fast fake, but not a subtle one. The receiver must stand to stutter abruptly enough to force the defender to react. This fake works best when it is executed at a point where the receiver has been making a successful pattern cut.

Shoulder Turn

This fake is also used to separate from a defender to run a deep route and is very similar to the change-of-pace fake. The receiver drives off the line of scrimmage to the depth where he wants to draw the defender. He will turn his head and shoulders in, as if he were about to run a turn or circle route. It is important that he does not turn the hips in, causing him to lose his downfield speed. After closing the defender's cushion, he will regain the proper sprinting form to beat him deep.

Angle of Release

The receiver can work for separation even as he releases from the line. By quickly gaining a yard of lateral separation from the defender prior to the cut, still greater separation is made after the break (Diagram 6-2).

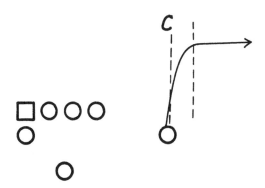

Diagram 6-2

Jab

The jab is used to force a defender to keep his cushion. It is particularly useful on a smooth, bending route, such as the circle route. Just prior to making his cut, the receiver can jab-step upfield at the deep defender to keep him playing soft. The jab upfield is quick and there is very little loss of speed to the inside seam.

PRINCIPLES OF CATCHING

Concentration

The technique of fine-tuning his concentration to the football is a receiver's most valuable skill. Only when his mind is focused completely on the ball will his developed skill work naturally to produce consistent and fluid receptions.

From the time the eyes pick the ball up in flight until it is secured, the receiver's total concentration must be on the ball. The mind can concentrate completely on just one thing at a time. By learning the skill of concentration, the receiver's performance will not be hampered by additional thoughts of past experiences or anticipation. Both detract from a fluid reception of a class performer.

If the receiver fails to keep his thoughts focused on the ball in flight, he will be subject to thoughts such as, "I can't let myself miss this easy one," or "The linebacker is going to hit me right in the mouth just after I catch this ball." The results of such thoughts are all the same. The receiver's natural talent that has been developed over a period of years is inhibited. He is rigid and is unnatural in his attempt. But if he can learn to fine-tune his total concentration onto the football, his thoughts won't be allowed to wander. His reception will be smooth and natural. If he is in a crowd, the eyes will pull him to the ball, and he will protect both the ball and himself in a natural way.

With total concentration, the ball will appear to be even bigger and to be traveling slower. Hitting against a high-speed pitching machine is a good example of this. At first the ball seems to zip by, unable to be hit. But as the batter's concentration becomes focused, he finds his eyes can follow the ball, and the task of hitting it is not as difficult as it first appeared.

Concentration is fine-tuned by the receiver focusing on a small point on the ball. It can be the center of the tip of the football or the grain of the leather, or even the pattern of the seams. But it must be small, and the receiver must develop interest in it to hold his attention. With the concentration point identified, he will simply direct his attention and interest to it and let the mind fine-tune itself. He cannot force it. He cannot strain to make it happen. He must just let it flow.

This technique is developed like all others—through quality repetition. It can be practiced on every reception from the first warmup catch to the last one thrown his way in team period. Eventually, this concentration technique will become second nature as he achieves his best performance. If in practice or a game he feels it slipping away, he will need only to consciously bring his attention back to the concentration point.

Hand Position

If the shoulders are turned toward the ball, and the ball is armpit level or above, the thumbs should be turned in when making a catch. When the ball is below this level, or the shoulders are turned away from the ball, the thumbs should be turned out for this catch. In the gray areas between these catches, the receiver will find what is most natural for him through repetition.

Cushioning the Ball

The hands must cushion the ball for every type of catch. Passes to the body, or even wobbly passes, can best be caught with the hands in the proper position. The grip is firm and tacky, not rigid. A receiver can quickly develop this firm, tacky grip by seeing and feeling his catches in warmup. As the ball meets his hands, he will need only to switch his concentration to the feel of the reception and then look closely at his hand position. Through repetition the hands will adjust naturally to provide the proper cushion.

Building a Backup

Whenever possible, a pocket should be formed to provide a backup for the hands. For example, whenever going to the ground for a thumbs-out catch, the elbows should be brought close together so that if the receiver misses the ball with his hands, he will have it trapped between his arms and trunk.

Secure the Ball

The ball must be secured the instant it is caught. The fingers are spread over the front with its tip locked between the index and middle fingers, pulling the ball up and back to the rib cage, pressed inward to lock in the rear of the football. Whenever possible, it should be held on the side away from a potential tackler.

RUNNING WITH THE BALL

After the catch, the receiver must hit a seam and get quick upfield yardage. He should run with the balance and power necessary to break through arm tackles. He should run with the body lean necessary to penetrate through seams. Outmaneuvering defenders in the open field is valuable, but getting upfield with speed is the important point.

A back must be particularly aware of the seams between defenders. Nearly every catch he will make will be made underneath the undercover. It becomes critical for him to locate these seams between the undercover defenders and to hit these creases with power. In practice he must develop the skill of hitting with low shoulders between two tacklers. Getting his shoulders underneath the tacklers' force and keeping his legs driving will get the extra yards. A ball control pass offense demands this of its backs (Diagram 6-3).

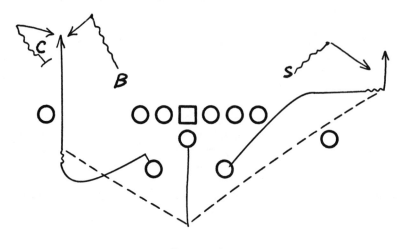

Diagram 6-3

Each receiver must be aware of the total picture. He should know where the first down is, where he will have blocking help, and how far he must go to get out-of-bounds to stop the clock.

Chapter 7

INDIVIDUAL ROUTES

FOR THE AIR OPTION

WIDE RECEIVER ROUTES

To be successful, a wide receiver must accomplish two objectives in running his route. First, he should force the defender out of position to stop the offensive play. Next, he must provide a consistent target for his quarterback.

Step count routes provide the wide receiver with the design to meet both of these requirements. With step count routes, a change of direction can be made with a specific number of steps. It can be designed to threaten an area of the defender's responsibility, forcing him out of position to defend against the route. Also, because step count routes are mapped out with a definite number of steps, the wide receiver can be exact in the execution of his route. A major factor in the proficiency of a passing game is the quarterback seeing consistent routes with which he can zero in his concentration and sharpen his timing and accuracy.

PATTERN STEM

The ability to go deep is a receiver's most dangerous weapon. Each route that the wide receiver runs should have this threat built into it. Without this threat, the man-to-man defender on the deep zone defender can make light of his deep responsibility and shut off the medium passing game. The Air Option design utilized the go route and the post route as stems for its routes. The stem consists of the get-off, controlled run, and is followed by the route cut (Diagram 7-1).

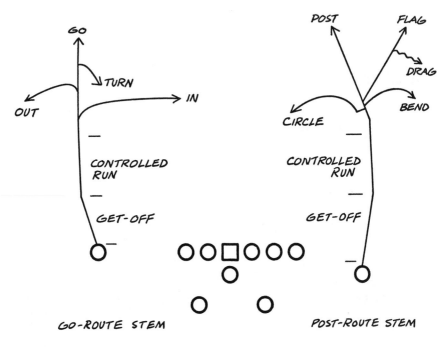

Diagram 7-1

Get-Off

The receiver's four-step get-off should force the defender to get deep in a hurry or lose his cushion. From his stance a complete and forceful extension of his drive leg and hip will start this explosive get-off. There should be good body lean and forceful arm-and-leg action. Each receiver will find the proper balance between his length and rate of stride through experimentation.

Controlled Run

After the four-step get-off, the receiver will shift into the controlled run that he will be in until his route cut. The controlled run does not mean that he slows down, rather he simply switches from the acceleration of the get-off to a run that is balanced, smooth, and relaxed. He should be controlled enough to make a crisp route cut.

In this controlled run, he will also set up the defender to get the best position to make his cut. He should drive to a position where his movement out of the cut will increase his separation from the defender (Diagram 7-2).

The cut is made off the opposite foot of the direction the receiver intends to go. It is initiated with the next to the last step, breaking his speed. He should not lean back and throw his arms back when preparing to make the cut as if to tell the defender, "I'm making a sideline cut now." Rather, the arms and body should be kept in as normal a running position as possible.

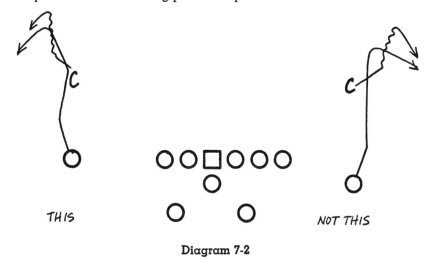

Diagram 7-2

The actual cut is made off a slightly bent knee. The foot is planted heel-toe, and the bent knee absorbs most of the force of the cut. The back is slightly bent with the weight slightly in back of the supporting bent knee. If the receiver's complete concentration is on receiving the football, his head and shoulders will naturally snap around to see the ball on the cut.

The first step after the cut should put the receiver as near as possible in the direction he intends to go. However, he cannot afford to cut so sharply that he stalls out in the middle of the cut. As he improves his bent-knee cutting technique, he will get closer and closer to the correct angle on his first step.

When a speed cut is indicated for a particular route, the emphasis will be on the speed coming out of the cut rather than the sharpness of it. The same basic technique is used, but now the receiver will roll through the cut, and it will not be as precise.

The bent-knee technique for cutting is much better than the often used straight leg cut. It lowers the center of gravity, giving the receiver improved stability. The bent knee absorbs the impact of the cut, eliminating slipping, and it keeps the body bent over, preventing the defensive back from keying when the receiver is going to make a cut. The bent knee also lends itself to a greater speed coming out of the cut because it can be extended and generate force.

POST STEM ROUTES

The five basic routes that come off of the post stem are the post, bend, circle, flag, and drag.

Post Route

The receiver explodes off the line of scrimmage for four steps, aiming for the cornerback's outside shoulder. The next three strides are controlled strides and are straight upfield (Diagram 7-3).

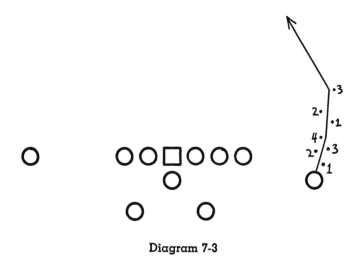

Diagram 7-3

After these seven strides, the receiver uses a speed cut (sometimes referred to as the "stick") inside the defender to the post. He should have a stride on the defender at this point, and if the ball is thrown to stretch the receiver downfield, a touchdown or long gain is the reward. It is very important that the receiver breaks just inside of the cornerback to stay in the seam, away from the free safety.

Key Adjustments to Coverage

Versus Rotation: The wide receiver should slip tight to the inside of the rotating cornerback. He cannot be delayed or lose his width by being funneled too far to the inside. Once by the cornerback, he will run his post cut on the deep outside one-third defender. Against two deep zone, the receiver should try to stretch the deep half defender before breaking to the post, slipping by him to the inside (Diagram 7-4).

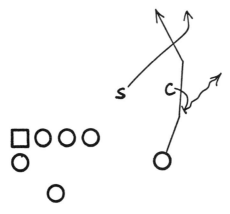

Diagram 7-4

Versus Bump and Run: A quick outside release and speed to get over the top of the cornerback is critical. Once the corner is beaten, the receiver can run his post cut on the deep one-third or deep half defender (Diagram 7-5).

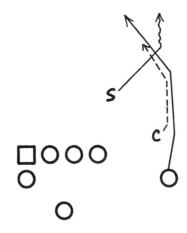

Diagram 7-5

Versus Double Zone (Inside-Outside): After making his post cut, the wide receiver may have to use a shoulder turn inside to hold the inside defender momentarily. This will allow him to beat the defender over the top after he splits the bracket (Diagram 7-6).

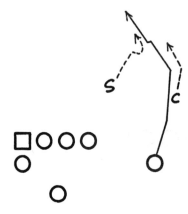

Diagram 7-6

Bend Route

The wide receiver begins by running the Post stem. He should duplicate the release and controlled run of the Post route. Next he will break to the post for three strides. This post move or "stick" should soften the defender and cause him to shift his weight back and to the inside. On the third step of the post move, the receiver will make a speed cut to the sideline with the eyes swinging around toward the ball releasing out of the quarterback's hand. With full concentration on the tip of the football, after snapping his head around, he must hug back to meet the ball. Coming back to the ball lengthens the distance between the receiver and the defender and improves the throwing-catching angle. The ball will be caught about 17 yards deep (Diagram 7-7).

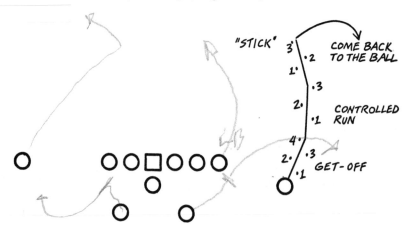

Diagram 7-7

Key Adjustments to Coverage

Versus Rotation: The wide receiver must get a quick outside release and then hang in the seam between the rotating cornerback and the deep outside one-third or deep half defender. This route will probably be taken away by this coverage. However, by stretching the coverage with an outside release, he will open a seam for an inside receiver (Diagram 7-8).

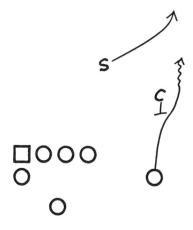

Diagram 7-8

Versus Bump and Run: The wide receiver must get a quick outside release and then really threaten deep with his post break. This stick to the post will get the cornerback running to where it will be impossible for him to defend against a good out-break on the bend route (Diagram 7-9).

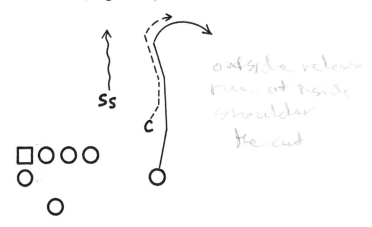

Diagram 7-9

Versus Double Zone (Inside-Outside): The wide receiver must first do an adequate job threatening the post to soften the outside defender. Next, he must be ready to cut just a little harder to bend back and in front of the defender to his outside (Diagram 7-10).

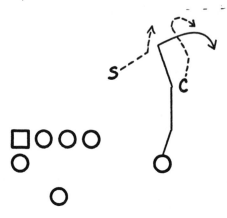

Diagram 7-10

Circle Route

As the wide receiver is in the controlled area of the post stem, he should key undercover to see where the throwing lane is going to be. As he breaks into the post move, he will either circle to an open inside seam or hook up in an open outside seam, depending on the coverage. If there is no one threatening the outside throwing lane, he will hook up on the second step of his post move and come straight back to meet the ball. If there is a defender in the outside throwing lane, he will speed cut to the next inside throwing lane, again coming back to meet the ball (Diagram 7-11).

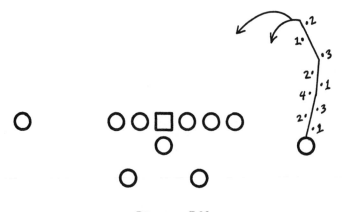

Diagram 7-11

Key Adjustments to Coverage

Versus Rotation: The wide receiver should slip tight to the inside of the rotating cornerback. He cannot lose his lanes to the inside by being funneled down (Diagram 7-12).

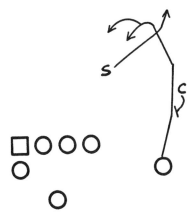

Diagram 7-12

Versus Bump and Run: Speed to get on top ot the defender is critical. Once on top, the receiver will need only to jab out and then snap back around to separate from his defender (Diagram 7-13).

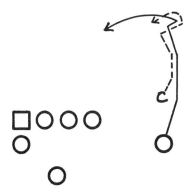

Diagram 7-13

Versus Double Zone: It is important for the wide receiver to do a good job threatening the post. He must soften his inside defender before working hard back to the inside on his circle route (Diagram 7-14).

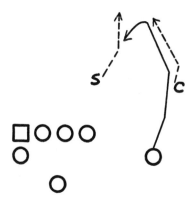

Diagram 7-14

Flag Route

The flat route begins with the post stem pulling the defender in with him. On the third step of the post move, the receiver cuts back to the outside of the defender to the flag. Because the defender must shift his weight to cross back to the outside, the receiver will have a stride on him. After the break, the receiver will snap his eyes over the outside shoulder with total concentration on the ball. It is important that he hold his course as he comes out of his cut. The quarterback will be throwing on time and unless the receiver holds his line, it will be impossible to judge the receiver's direction and complete the pass (Diagram 7-15).

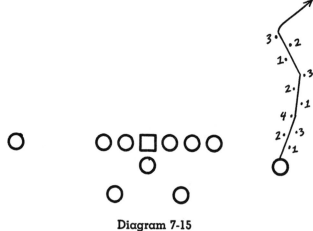

Diagram 7-15

Key Adjustments to Coverage

Versus Rotation: The wide receiver should slip tight to the inside of the rotating cornerback. He cannot be delayed or funneled or lose too much width by being funneled too far to the inside. Once by the cornerback, he will adjust his flag to a drag route. First he will drive to the corner, and then roll off to the sideline (Diagram 7-16).

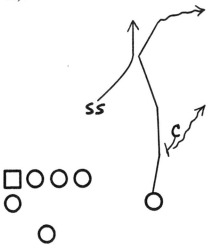

Diagram 7-16

Versus Bump and Run: As with the bend route, the wide receiver must get a quick outside release and then really threaten deep with his post move. This "stick" to the post will get the cornerback running and will make it very difficult for him to cover the receiver running the corner and then bending it off to a drag route (Diagram 7-17).

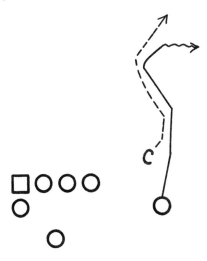

Diagram 7-17

Versus Double Zone: The wide receiver must do a good job driving to the corner to soften his outside defender before adjusting his route to a drag route.

Drag Route

This route begins exactly like the flag route. After the get-off, controlled run, and three-step post move, the receiver breaks to the flag. Just as he starts towards the flag, he will roll the route off to the sideline and come back slightly to meet the ball, 24 yards deep on the sideline. The ball should be thrown to stretch the receiver to the sideline (Diagram 7-18).

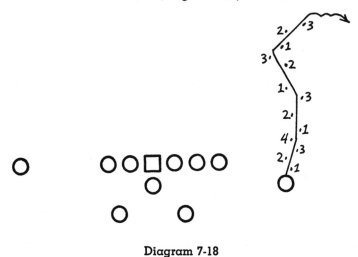

Diagram 7-18

Key Adjustments to Coverage

The adjustments for the drag route are the same as for the flag.

GO STEM ROUTES

The four basic routes that come off the go stem are the go, turn, out, and in.

Go Route

The receiver explodes off the line of scrimmage for four steps, aiming at the cornerback's outside shoulder. After his release, he turns straight upfield on a full sprint to break by the deep defender's outside or inside shoulder. Breaking by the defender's outside is the preferred way to run the route, but the inside break must be used against a defender who has taken a definite outside position. It is important that the receiver breaks close by the defender to prevent him from covering this deep route with a good cut-off angle. The ball should be thrown over the receiver's outside shoulder where he can fade late on the ball but still catch it over his inside shoulder. If the receiver is just even with the defender, a well-thrown ball and the late fade make this pattern very difficult to defend. It is important to know exactly the distance of the quarterback's range. Tommy Kramer at Rice was a 45-yard deep passer. Greg Cook at Cincinnati was a 65-yard deep passer. The distance for the receiver is important so as not to outrun or under-run his passer (Diagram 7-19).

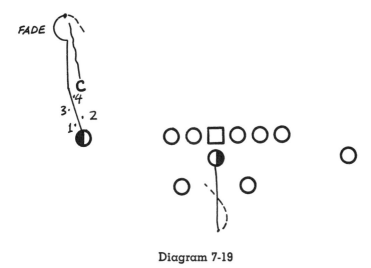

Diagram 7-19

Key Adjustments to Coverage

Versus Rotation: The wide receiver must get a quick outside release and then be ready to hang in the seam between the rotating cornerback and the deep outside one-third or deep half defender (Diagram 7-20).

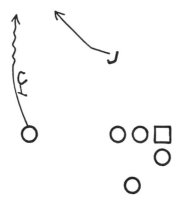

Diagram 7-20

Versus Bump and Run: The wide receiver should slip tight to the outside of the cornerback, utilizing the fade technique when the ball arrives (Diagram 7-21).

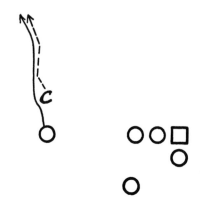

Diagram 7-21

Versus Double Zone: The wide receiver should stretch the outside defender. If the defender fails to maintain outside position, the receiver should slip him tight to the outside. If the defender maintains this outside position, he should sprint and slip by tight to the defender inside (Diagram 7-22).

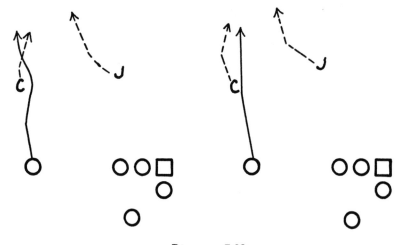

Diagram 7-22

Turn Route

This route begins just like the go route. The receiver releases at the outside shoulder of the cornerback and then attacks upfield as though he were going to run a go route. As he drives upfield, he should move to an inside shoulder position on the defender. With this position, his turn to his inside will carry him away from the defender. On the eleventh step of his route, the receiver will plant a bent-knee cut and hook. The eleventh step will take him about 18 yards deep. If an undercover defender is in the throwing lane, the receiver should run to split the nearest seam while coming back quickly to meet the ball (Diagram 7-23).

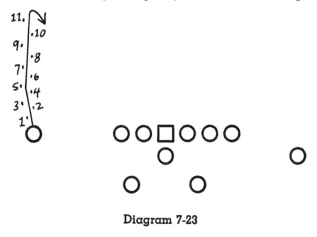

Diagram 7-23

Key Adjustments to Coverage

Versus Rotation: The wide receiver should slip tight to the inside of the rotating cornerback. He cannot lose his lanes to the inside by being funneled down (Diagram 7-24).

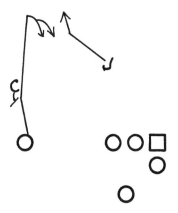

Diagram 7-24

Versus Bump and Run: He should take a quick outside release and sprint to threaten the go route. On the eleventh step of the route, he will plant hook and slide hard to the outside away from the defender's inside position (Diagram 7-25).

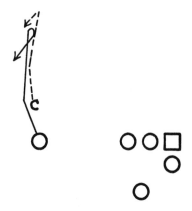

Diagram 7-25

Versus Double Zone: The wide receiver should release to stretch the outside defender. On his eleventh step, he will plant and work back, staying between the two bracket defenders. Usually this will require him to work straight back upfield (Diagram 7-26).

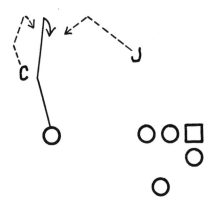

Diagram 7-26

Out Route

This route begins just like the go route. The get-off and controlled run should sell the go. Late into his controlled run, the receiver should move to an outside shoulder position on the defender so that the out cut will break him away from the defender. On the tenth step of his route he will make a speed cut to the outside and work back slightly to meet the ball (Diagram 7-27).

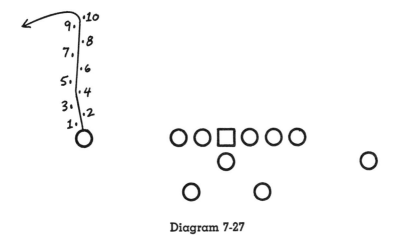

Diagram 7-27

Key Adjustments to Coverage

Versus Rotation: The wide receiver must get a quick outside release and then hang in the seam between the rotating cornerback and the deep outside one-third or deep half defender. This route will probably be taken away by his coverage. However, by stretching the coverage with an outside release, he will open a seam for an inside receiver (Diagram 7-28).

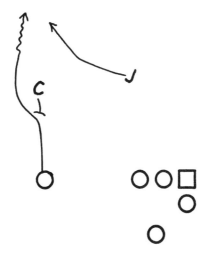

Diagram 7-28

Versus Bump and Run: He should take a quick outside release and sprint to threaten the go route. Late into the route, he should lean heavily to his inside and threaten going over the top of the defender. On his tenth step, he will break hard and back to the outside (Diagram 7-29).

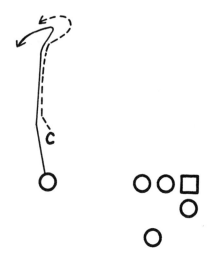

Diagram 7-29

Versus Double Zone: The wide receiver will take his normal course until his eighth step. On his eighth step, he will drive at his outside defender for two steps to get a head-up position. On his *tenth step, he will break hard and back to the outside* (Diagram 7-30).

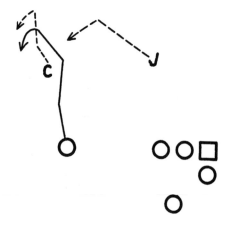

Diagram 7-30

In Route

Again the receiver begins this pattern as though it were a go route to threaten the defender deep. After his outside release, he continues to drive at the defender's outside shoulder to spread the coverage and perhaps turn the defender. Late into the controlled run he shifts to an inside shoulder position on the defender, and on his ninth step makes a speed cut to the inside. As he continues across in a controlled run, he must search for a throwing lane in the undercover. When he hits it, he will idle down and hug back slightly to the passer (Diagram 7-31).

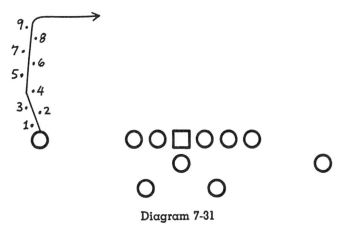

Diagram 7-31

Key Adjustments to Coverage

Versus Rotation: The wide receiver should slip tight to the inside of the rotating cornerback. He cannot lose the lanes to his inside by being funneled down (Diagram 7-32).

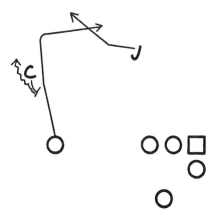

Diagram 7-32

Versus Bump and Run: Speed to get on top of the defender is critical. Once on top, the receiver will need only to jab out and then snap back around to separate from his defender (Diagram 7-33).

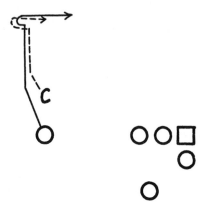

Diagram 7-33

Versus Double Zone: The route will be adjusted to a post in. On the seventh step of his route, he will drive to the post for two strides to soften the inside defender. On the ninth step, he will break flat to come under his inside defender (Diagram 7-34).

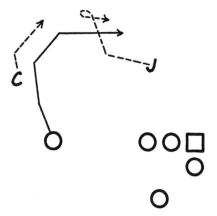

Diagram 7-34

QUICK ROUTES

There are two pass routes used by the wide receiver to break off the first four steps (get-off) of the stem. These routes will be run in combination with a three-step dropback by the quarterback. These routes will give the receiver a way to take advantage of quick, soft defenders or when a short zone is poorly defended.

Quick Out

Striding first with the outside leg, the receiver drives four steps at the defender's outside shoulder. On the fourth step, he will make a speed cut to the sideline. By concentrating solely on the flight of the ball, his head and shoulders will snap around to quickly see the ball. At this depth there is no need to hug back to meet the ball. With proper timing the receiver will catch the ball in stride at about 6 yards deep, turning up the sideline (Diagram 7-35).

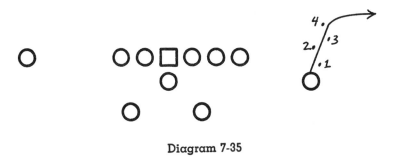

Diagram 7-35

Key Adjustments to Coverage

Versus Rotation: The wide receiver must get a quick outside release and then hang in the seam between the rotating cornerback and the deep outside one-third or deep half defender. This route will probably be taken away by this coverage. However, by stretching the coverage with an outside release, he will open a seam for an inside receiver (Diagram 7-36).

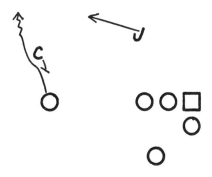

Diagram 7-36

Versus Bump and Run: He should take a tight outside release and lean on his defender. On his fourth step, he should break sharply away from his defender.

Quick Slant

On the third step of the get-off, the receiver will make a speed cut to the inside. The angle and depth must be adjusted to the coverage. The shoulders should be opened to face the quarterback so that the receiver is in the best possible position to react to the ball and to give the quarterback a good target. This pattern can become one of the most effective pass routes in the entire package. The quarterback can vary his drop by backpedaling because he may need more depth in relation to the coverage. Tommy Kramer at Rice became a master of the controlled drop in executing this pattern (Diagram 7-37).

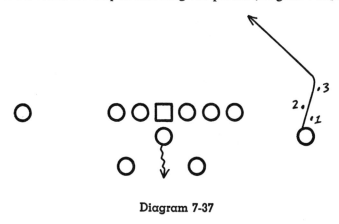

Diagram 7-37

Key Adjustments to Coverage

Versus Bump and Run: His release is everything. He will use either a head-fake and rip or a head-butt release. Whichever he uses, he must get quickly to the inside of his defender with enough separation for a reception.

TIGHT END ROUTES (DIAGRAM 7-38)

Streak Route

The tight end takes an inside release and sprints straight upfield, looking for the ball over his inside shoulder. He cannot be delayed on the line of scrimmage, and he cannot get funneled off course. As with the wide receiver's go route, it is important that the tight end break close by a man-to-man defender to prevent him from covering the pass with a good cut-off angle.

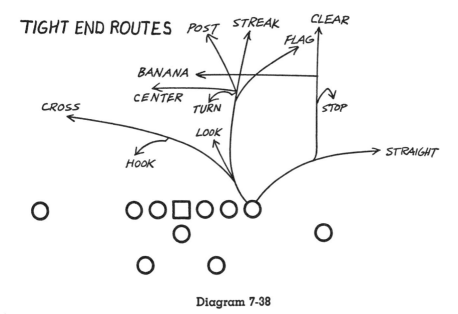

Diagram 7-38

Turn Route

The tight end takes an inside release and sprints straight upfield to sell the streak route. He cannot let the defender funnel him too far inside on his release. That would squeeze down the area that he will have to get open.

As he attacks upfield to soften the deep coverage, he must key the undercover to see where the throwing lane is going to be. At a depth of 12 yards, he will turn to the open lane showing his "numbers" to the quarterback.

Post Route

The tight end takes an inside release to a depth of 12 yards before making the post break. He will use a speed cut and maintain maximum speed and pressure on the deep third defender. Against a man-to-man defender, he will need to drive at the defender's outside shoulder to spread the coverage. As he closes on the defender, he should then drive at his inside shoulder before breaking on his post cut.

Corner Route

This route begins just like the post route. After taking an inside release, the tight end will drive to a depth of 12 yards. At that depth he will make a speed cut to the corner. It is important for the accuracy of the pass that he hold a straight line after his cut. Against man-to-man coverage, he should jab-step to the inside just before the cut. This will turn the defender and allow the tight end to gain a step or more on the defender.

Center Route

The tight end takes an inside release and sprints straight upfield to a depth of 12 yards. At that depth he will make a speed cut to the inside. As he continues across, he will search for a throwing lane. When he hits the lane, he should hug back slightly to make the catch.

Clear Route

The tight end takes an outside release and sprints straight upfield, looking for the ball over his inside shoulder. This is basically a deep control route. He must get quick pressure on the deep coverage. He cannot be delayed on the line of scrimmage.

Stop Route

On this route the tight end takes a tight outside release and then drives upfield to "sell" the clear route. He cannot let the defender funnel him too wide on his release. By holding his upfield line he will have room to the outside to slide and get open.

At 12 yards depth he will hook to the outside, break into a seam in the undercover. As he works back to meet the ball, he should move quickly to split zone defenders.

Banana Route

Again, the tight end takes a tight outside release and drives upfield to sell the clear route. At a depth of 15 yards, he will make a speed cut to the inside. As he continues across in a controlled run, he must search for a throwing lane in the undercoverage. When he hits the lane, he should hug back slightly to make the catch.

Straight Route

The tight end takes a straight outside release, aiming for a point 6 yards deep on the sideline. This is a speed route designed to hold the flat zone defender. On his release he should look for the ball over his outside shoulder. He will be gaining depth as he sprints to the flat. If the ball is not thrown to him on his route, he should hold up 2 yards from the sideline and turn to face the quarterback to act as a late outlet.

Look Route

The tight end takes a tight inside release, looking quickly for the ball. He cannot be funneled to the inside. His strong upfield movement should take him on a course outside the inside linebacker's drop.

Cross Route

This route is designed to get the tight end 17 yards deep in the opposite flat zone. The tight end takes a quick inside release and works for depth as he crosses the field. He will have to look in order to avoid being delayed or funneled off course by undercover defenders.

Hook Route

This route begins just like the cross route. After taking a quick inside release, he will start across the formation, gaining depth as he goes. When he is about even with the center, he should be about 10 yards deep. At that point he will plant and hug back to the passer. This is an aggressive control route. The tight end is to control the inside linebacker drops and yet fight to get open in front of their drops or in seams between them.

BACKFIELD ROUTES (DIAGRAM 7-39)

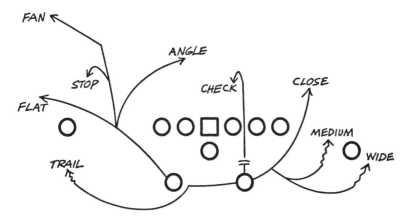

Diagram 7-39

Wide Route

To run the wide route, the back jab-steps at his pass blocking assignment and then runs an arc through the wide receiver's alignment. By bellying back to a depth of 6 yards off the line of scrimmage and then bending his route forward, he will be in a good position to open his shoulders to the quarterback for an easy reception. Heading upfield also allows him to move quickly downfield after the catch. He should get as wide as the wide receiver and make the catch from 2 to 4 yards off the line of scrimmage. The back should sprint for width and then idle down to come under control as he nears the catching point.

Medium Route

The back begins the medium route as though he were running the wide route. After his jab step to check his pass blocking assignment, he bellies back to 6 yards off the line of scrimmage. Next, he bends his route forward so that it arcs through a point that splits the wide receiver and the offensive tackle. He must idle down the route so that he is on the line of scrimmage to time himself with the quarterback's delivery.

Close Route

After stepping up to check his blocking assignment, the back releases just outside the offensive tackle. He cannot get so close to the tackle that there is a chance of knocking him off his block. As he approaches the line of scrimmage, he breaks straight upfield looking for the ball over his inside shoulder. This route is often a clearing route. The back cannot be delayed on his release.

Trail Route

On the snap, the back sprints flat across the formation to a position behind the offensive guard. From this position he simply runs a wide or medium route, depending upon the pass play called.

Flat Route

After the jab step at his blocking assignment, the back sprints 5 yards downfield for a point that splits the wide receiver and the offensive tackle. It is a full-speed sprint, and at that point breaks flat to the sideline. On the break, he brings his head smoothly around to see the quarterback and opens his shoulders slightly to provide a better target. This will also put him in a good position to react to the pass. If the ball is not thrown to him by the time he nears the sideline, he should hold up 2 yards from the sideline and turn to face the quarterback.

Stop Route

This route begins just like the flat route. The receiver sprints for the point 5 yards downfield and midway between the wide receiver and offensive tackle. At that point he turns straight upfield and to a depth of 8 yards and then hooks outside to face the quarterback. As he cuts, he should bring his eyes quickly around to see the quarterback.

Fan Route

This route begins as the stop route. The receiver sprints for the point 5 yards downfield and midway between the wide receiver and offensive tackle. At that point he turns straight upfield and drives to a depth of 12 yards. At that depth he will angle out, aiming for a point 17 yards deep on the sideline. Versus man coverage, he may need to use jab to the inside before making his final break to separate from his defender.

Angle Route

This route also begins as a flat route. The back's initial direction is for a point 5 yards downfield and midway between the wide receiver and offensive tackle. As he approaches the line of scrimmage, he will break back over the middle, crossing the formation at a depth of 6 yards. The game plan may dictate that he look up after he gets his depth.

Check Route

On this route the back delays a count and a half before hooking 5 yards deep in front of his offensive guard. His technique is to step at his pass blocking assignment and delay to let the coverage drop, and then release through an open lane to his set-up point. He must be careful not to knock an offensive lineman off his block as he releases through the line. When he gets to his 6-yard breaking point, he plants his outside foot and hooks quickly to the inside to face the quarterback. This check route may also be run after a draw fake.

Chapter 8

RECEIVER

DEVELOPMENT

A receiver's top performance is a result of his natural ability, and the quality of the work that he has done to improve his skills. He cannot change his natural ability, so his improvement must come from skill development. It is critical that he understands that his skills are habits, and that consistent performance comes about by grooming his skills through quality repetition.

RECEIVER SEQUENCE

The receiver sequence is a series of drills designed to give the needed repetitions on these skills. It should be integrated into the in-season practice schedule as well as three days a week in the off-season.

Ball Security Drills

Turning the ball over to the opponent with a fumble is perhaps the most devastating thing that can happen to a football team. Before a team stands a chance of winning, it must first learn how not to beat itself. By doing these ball security drills, the receivers will learn how to protect the ball and never fumble.

Each drill is started with the football properly secured. There is a tight squeeze on the front and rear of the football. The fingers are spread over the front with its tip locked between the index and middle fingers. It is pulled up and back to the rib cage to secure as much of it as possible. The elbow is pressed inward to lock in the rear of the football.

Secure the Ball: The receiver squeezes the ball in an isometric contraction of 15 seconds for each arm. As he squeezes, he will feel every point of the secure hold.

Wrestle the Ball: With the ball well secured, two receivers will yank at one another's football several times, trying to dislodge it.

Monkey Roll with the Ball: With the ball properly secured, Player A will side-roll to his left. As he approaches, Player B will hop over him and side-roll to his right. As Player B approaches, Player C will hop over him and side-roll to his left. The drill continues in this manner until the coach gives the command to stop (Diagram 8-1).

Diagram 8-1

Ball Handling Drills

The ball handling drills are used to help the receiver improve his hands and develop familiarity and confidence in handling the football. While doing the drills, the ball should not be gripped too tightly. Rather, it should be controlled with a firm, tacky grip.

Air Dribble: With one hand the receiver tosses the ball and catches it with the palm facing down, similar to the action in dribbling a basketball (15 seconds with each hand).

Circle the Ball and Catch: With palm facing down, the receiver will drop the ball, quickly circle it with the hand in a clockwise direction, and catch it again with the palm facing down (15 seconds each hand).

Move the Ball: The receiver passes the ball behind his back and between his legs from one hand to the other in quick movements (15 seconds each hand).

Globe-Trotter: The receiver combines all ball handling stunts into a routine of quick ball handling movements. There are a number of other stunts that the receiver will develop through experimentation. All of these can be worked into the routine (15 seconds).

Catching Drills

Check Hand Position (20 catches): In this drill the receiver works to perfect hand positioning while developing concentration on the ball. At a distance of 12 yards he will stand facing a passer. By passing the ball high, low, wide, and close to the body, the passer will give the receiver the variety of passes he needs to drill for correct hand position on his reception. He will check hand-and-finger position, his back-up pocket, and secure the ball instantly.

He must first fasten his concentration on the tip of the football to insure the complete concentration necessary to be a consistent receiver. Upon the reception, he will shift his concentration to his hand position.

The passer will be sure to work the ball to all areas within the receiver's reach. Next, he will stand with his back to the passer, catching passes over each shoulder, again checking the same coaching points.

High Hook/Scoop Catch (two catches from each side for each type of catch): This drill will aid the receiver in developing the technique of catching the very high pass or the very low pass on the circle or turn routes (Diagram 8-2).

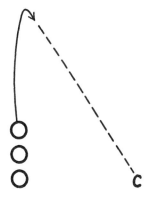

Diagram 8-2

The receiver will run downfield just two steps and circle or turn. The passer will throw high or low enough to challenge the receiver. On the scoop the receiver should build a backup with the elbows close together. Both of his hands must secure the ball as he hits the ground with the good scoop technique.

High in Front, Low in Front, Behind (two catches each side for each type of catch): The receiver turns 10 yards in front of the passer who will throw one of the three types of passes. Proper hand position, the timing of jumps or dives, the building of a backup, securing the ball as he hits the ground—every check point should be drilled to perfection (Diagram 8-3).

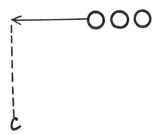

Diagram 8-3

Harassment Catch (two catches each side): The harassers will shove and pull the receiver as the receiver runs on line 10 yards in front of the passer (Diagram 8-4). Protecting the ball with the body, the building of a back-up and moving to the ball, and great concentration are prime coaching points for this drill.

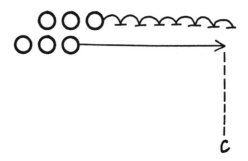

Diagram 8-4

Crisscross Distraction (two catches each side): This drill will give the receiver an opportunity to develop the concentration necessary for receiving a pass with a defender crossing in front of him (Diagram 8-5). He will run behind a distracter who is moving in the opposite direction. The passer will stand 10 yards from the receiver and throw the ball through the distracter to the receiver.

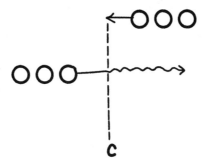

Diagram 8-5

Hands-Up Distraction (two catches each side): This drill will give the receiver an opportunity to develop the concentration necessary for receiving behind undercoverage (Diagram 8-6). He will run behind a line of players who have their hands up trying to distract the receiver from the ball. All types of passes will be thrown. Learning to use a concentration point on the ball is the key to the reception.

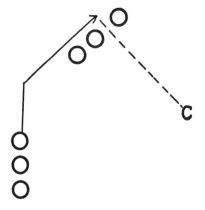

Diagram 8-6

Over-the-Shoulder and Wrong-Shoulder Catch (two catches each side) (Diagram 8-7): The passer should throw short, medium, and long passes of varied areas and angles, and even over the wrong shoulder. The key coaching point is to maintain good running form and let the receiver's concentration on the ball control his movement to the ball.

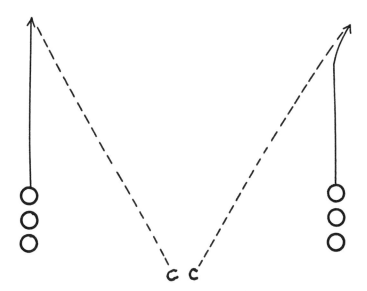

Diagram 8-7

One-Man Concentration (two catches each side): The receiver will develop both concentration and the technique of securing the ball quickly as he is being hit (Diagram 8-8).

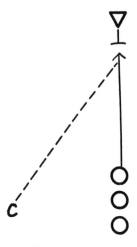

Diagram 8-8

One player with an air bag will stand 10 yards away, facing the receiver. The receiver comes off the line full speed, and the ball is thrown at the last moment. The receiver will make the reception and secure the ball just before the collision. Just after he makes the catch, the bag holder will unload on him.

Sideline Catch (two catches each side) (Diagram 8-9): The receiver splits 8 yards from the sideline and runs a quick out. The passer will stand at the normal launch point and throw the ball so that the receiver must stretch to make an

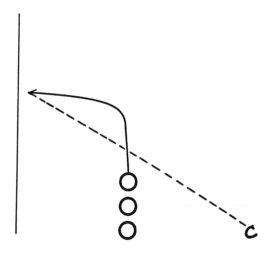

Diagram 8-9

inbounds catch. The passer will throw high and in front as well as low and in front passes. The receiver keeps his concentration on the ball. The feet will learn where the sideline is and how to stay inbounds.

End Zone Catch (two catches each side): Again the ball will be thrown so that the receiver must stretch to make an inbounds catch (Diagram 8-10).

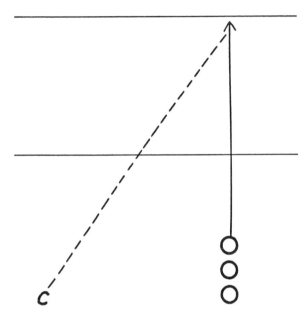

Diagram 8-10

Route Work

Stance and Get-Off (two times each side): The greatest threat a receiver has is the threat of going deep. He can improve this deep threat by developing an explosive release.

In this drill the receiver explodes off the line and accelerates for four strides. He will check his stance for the best position to explode off the line, and with a complete and forceful extension of the drive leg and hip, start an explosive release. Forceful arm-and-leg action, joined with good body lean and correct stride rate and length, are necessary for a good get-off.

Releases (two times each side for each release): In this drill the receiver simply works his shoot-out and arm-over releases to avoid being held up by a holdup defender.

Weave: The weave is a snakelike move in which the receiver makes 30-degree breaks every three steps. The move is smooth and is accomplished with a shift in body weight without any loss of speed. The weave is the fundamental drill that teaches the consistent rhythm of stride necessary to run step-count routes.

The receiver starts the drill by running the weave for 50 yards at half-speed and then three-quarter speed, and will finish with a full-speed weave.

Step Count: The receiver runs any three of his post-stemmed routes and any three of his go-stemmed routes two times from each side. He will alternate the routes each day so that each of his routes will be reviewed over the course of the week.

Chapter 9

THE AIR OPTION

SUPPLEMENT

T HE Air Option and its supplements can work hand-in-hand with practically any of the current running games to form a complete offensive package. The supplements include the lead draw, option screens, and play action passes.

THE LEAD DRAW

At times there is a need to help control the defensive pass rush. The draw concept is a very effective way to help control the inside rush—to give the defense something to think about other than their pass rush (Diagram 9-1).

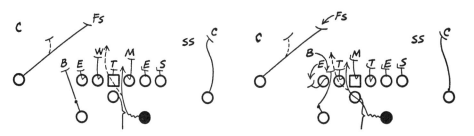

Diagram 9-1

Assignments

Split End: The split end will release directly for the free safety. However, if the cornerback becomes more of a threat to stop the play, the split end will pivot and block him

Flankerback: The flankerback simply runs a deep route. When the cornerback reacts to the draw, the flankerback will wall-block inside-out with a stutter block.

Tight End: The tight end will block through the inside shoulder of the end man on the line of scrimmage. The delay of the play demands that the tight end work hard to sustain his block and not lose his man to the inside.

Left Tackle: The left tackle will pick up his hand taking a short pass set and invite the defensive end to rush to the outside. If the defender does in fact rush outside, the tackle will need only to wall him out (Diagram 9-2). Should the defender rush to the inside, the tackle will have to drive him down the line of scrimmage to create an outside running lane (Diagram 9-3).

Diagram 9-2

Diagram 9-3

Left Guard: If there is a linebacker over him, the left guard will pick up his hand taking a short pass drop. This drop will help sell the draw and will put him in a better position to adjust to line stunts. After this short pass set, he will block the linebacker down the middle (Diagram 9-4).

If the left guard is covered by a defensive lineman, he will pick up his hand and take a very short pass drop to allow the defender to make a choice as to which side he wants to rush.

Diagram 9-4

Diagram 9-5

As soon as the defender declares his rush, the guard will attack, blocking him in the direction the defender wants to go. The ball carrier will be running off of his block (Diagram 9-5).

Center: When the center is covered by a defensive lineman, the ball carrier will run off of his block. On the snap, he will aggressively block the defender down the middle—he will not pass set.

When the center is covered by a linebacker, he will now take a short pass set before blocking through his defender's playside number. This pass set will serve the same purpose as it did for the guard when he was covered by a linebacker. The center must never get caught by a defensive line stunt—he should always option around (Diagram 9-6).

This is a run to daylight play for the running back, so it is important for the left tackle and guard to sustain their blocks. If the

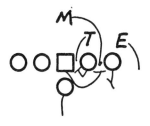

Diagram 9-6

defensive end or the defender playing over the center stunts to cut off his path to the linebacker, he will simply option around to block his assignment.

Right Guard: If there is a linebacker over him, the right guard is much like the left guard. He will pick up his hand and short-pass set to sell the draw and then block his linebacker down the middle. Because the ball carrier will be keying the center's block and then running to daylight, it is important that the guard stay square on his block. If he is covered by a defensive lineman, he will pick up his hand taking a very short pass set and invite an outside rush. Once the defender is outside, the guard will wall him out. It is important that he not over-position and allow a quick runaround.

Right Tackle: The right tackle will pick up his hand taking a short pass set to invite the defender to rush to the outside and then wall him out. He cannot allow the defender to cross his face—he must take the inside away.

Halfback: The halfback will take a slight pause as though he were setting for pass protection. At the same time, he will locate the outside linebacker to his side to determine his best course to block him. He will key his tackle's block and release to block his target right down the middle. He would like to release to the outside of the tackle if at all possible. However, should the tackle's defender take a very wide rush and/or the linebacker slides inside, the halfback leads inside the tackle to block his linebacker (Diagram 9-7).

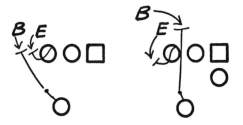

Diagram 9-7

Fullback: The fullback will take a short lateral slide to place him directly behind the right guard. From that position he will time his start forward with the quarterback's drop so that he will be moving forward as the ball is placed in his pocket.

Versus a 43 defensive front, his aiming point is for the tail of his left guard. He will sprint off that guard's block and run to daylight (Diagram 9-8).

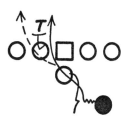

Diagram 9-8

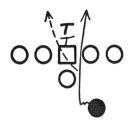

Diagram 9-9

He will key his center's block when running against a 34 defensive front (Diagram 9-9)

Quarterback: On the snap, the quarterback will begin his normal dropback. On the second step of his drop, he will snap his eyes directly to the belt buckle of his fullback. As he nears his fullback, he will extend his left hand and place the ball securely in the ball carrier's pocket. After his handoff, he will simply set up as if to pass.

This play can also be run to the strongside with the halfback carrying the football and the fullback leading. However, one of the most effective draws through the years has been the Lead Draw from the "I" formation. The assignments are similar except for the blocking on the weak side. Versus the 34 (odd spacing) front, the left tackle and left guard turn out on the defensive end and outside linebacker. The up back (fullback) takes a lateral step to his left and drives toward the linebacker over the left guard, blocking him down the middle (Diagram 9-10).

Against the 43 (even spacing) front, the fullback has the responsibility for the middle linebacker (Diagram 9-11).

The halfback (tailback in "I") now becomes the ball carrier. On the snap, the deep halfback takes a lateral step to the right and follows the same technique as previously described.

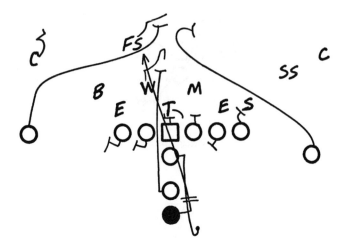

Diagram 9-10

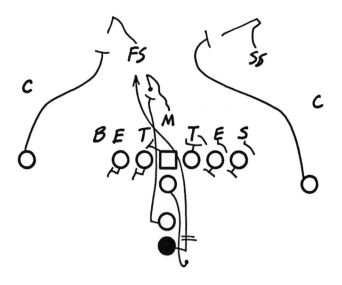

Diagram 9-11

SCREENS

The screen concept is another effective way to help control the defensive pass rush. The screens will give the defensive ends something else to think about other than laying their ears back and rushing the passer.

Option Screens

The option screen concept provides the quarterback with a primary receiver running a downfield route and a screening back positioned as an outlet. The quarterback simply options his pass in the same manner as any other of the Air Option patterns (Diagram 9-12).

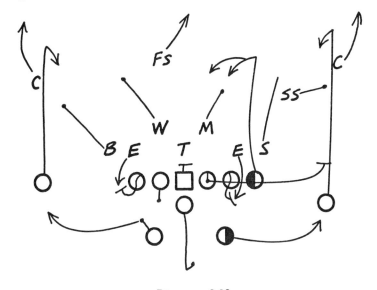

Diagram 9-12

Protection Assignments

The protection assignments for the linemen and the back that is aligned away from the screen are the same as 60 protection.

Option Screen Rules

The basic option screen rules call for the closest uncovered lineman to set short and release to the screen area when his assigned linebacker drops (Diagram 9-13). Should his linebacker dog, he will punch off to delay the rush before releasing to the screen area (Diagram 9-14).

A defensive line stunt that would ordinarily be switched must still be switched, and if it involves an uncovered lineman, the screen responsibility must

Diagram 9-13

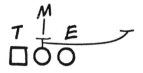

Diagram 9-14

Diagram 9-15

also be switched (Diagram 9-15). The screen area is in line with the wide receiver's alignment. The screening lineman simply pulls flat down the line to the screen area and leads upfield on the first defender who threatens the play. The screen relationship should allow the screen back to arc forward to catch the ball and be in line with his screening lineman.

Assignments

Split End and Flankerback: Both the split end and the flankerback will run a 12-yard stop route. To run the stop route, the receiver will release directly for his defender to his prescribed depth and simply pivot to face the quarterback.

This play calls for the quarterback to take a five-step drop and should he option his pass to his downfield route, the ball will be on its way as the receiver pivots (Diagram 9-16).

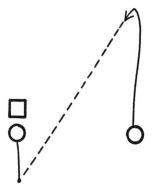

Diagram 9-16

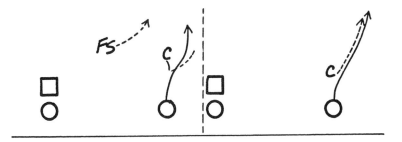

Diagram 9-17

Against a man-under defense or rotation, the receiver will fade his route to soften the coverage for the screen (Diagram 9-17).

Tight End: On an option screen to his side, the tight end will run a turn route at a depth of 12 yards. If he does not option the ball, he should turn and block the first defender in pursuit of the play.

Fullback: The fullback is the outlet and is the screening back. He does not have pass protection pickup—he is hot.

Should his linebacker dog, he will look quickly for the ball. The quarterback will also be keying that linebacker and will beat the rush by quickly delivering the ball off to the fullback (Diagram 9-18).

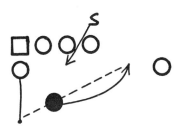

Diagram 9-18

If his assigned linebacker does not dog, he will run a wide route. The route is run under control at a moderate pace.

From the split formation he will belly back to a depth of 6 yards off the line of scrimmage before arcing forward through the wide receiver's alignment. He must come under control—turn his left shoulder so his numbers face the quarterback (Diagram 9-19).

A big key to the option screen being a highly productive play is the screening back's ability to attack quickly upfield after the

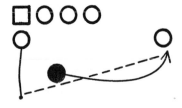

Diagram 9-19

catch. He must run with strength, balance, and a slashing style
that will allow him to run through arm tackles.

Quarterback: The quarterback takes a five-step drop and delivers his pass
to his primary receiver—the flankerback running the stop
route. Should the throwing lane to the flanker be threatened,
he will option his pass to his outlet receiver—the fullback
running the wide route.

Another key to the productivity of this play is the pass to the
screen back must pull the receiver slightly upfield. This
allows the fullback to get turned upfield without a delaying
stutter.

Option Screen Variations (Diagram 9-20)

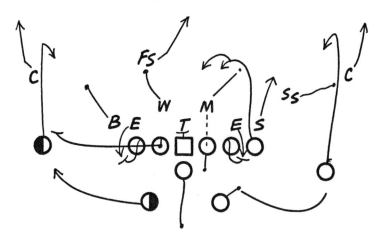

Diagram 9-20. 69 or 68 Stop-Wide Option Screen Weak

There are various types of screen philosophies. Through the years we have
experimented with practically every screen in existence. It takes precious practice time to develop a successful screen. In teaching the Air Option, we recom-
mended the option screen because it ties directly into the Air Option philosophy.
Anytime pulling linemen are involved, you will add extra hours to time out the
patterns.

PLAY ACTION PASSES

Play action passes serve an important function in the Air Option attack. To project a balanced offensive attack, an offense must be able to mix up its first down selections between the run and pass. The team with a 50 percent run and a 50 percent pass ratio on first down is completely balanced. This means the defense cannot benefit from a first down tendency report. The defense must prepare for both the run and pass. Many offensive teams have a high run ratio on first down and an almost 100 percent ratio when in backed-up territory. A defensive unit can load up its forces versus this type of attack. In the Air Option strategy, we mixed the run and pass on first down as close to a 50 percent ratio as the game plan allowed. The pass selections were divided between the backup passing game and play action passes. This type of mixture keeps the defense from guessing. It must defend against a balanced attack.

Other play action passes can be employed in these situations: short yardage situations, as a surprise element when a particular running play is gaining consistently, and in taking advantage of a single defender when vulnerable to a distinct action.

A play action pass can be designed from any running action in your system as long as the blocking scheme is sound, and the patterns relate to your Air Option routes.

Sweep Action

The sweep action possesses two play action passes with Air Option principles. In Diagram 9-21, the attack is designed toward formation to hold the strongside linebackers and the short outside zone.

The wide receiver on the formation side sprints deep to carry the deep one-third out of play. The tight end takes an inside release and drives deep to the

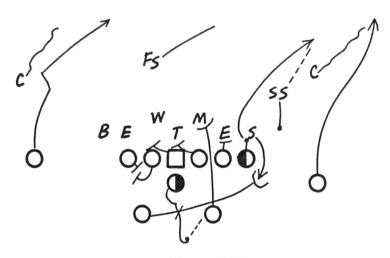

Diagram 9-21

corner. He is the primary receiver. However, the option develops from the free safety hustling to cover up the vacancy. Should this occur, the quarterback checks his release and drives the football to the wide receiver away from formation running the post route (Diagram 9-22).

Should the defensive secondary read pass and initially cover the tight-end, then he must use an inside head or shoulder fake at a depth of 12 yards and break away from his defender (Diagram 9-23).

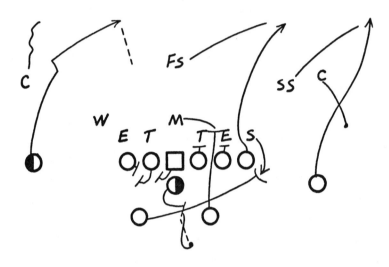

Diagram 9-22

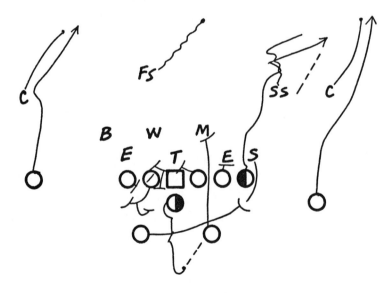

Diagram 9-23

The blocking scheme for the sweep action pass to the formation side is sound and allows full protection for the quarterback as he turns his head away from the line of scrimmage to carry out the faking action.

Assignments

Left Tackle: Set on defensive end. Use pocket protection technique.

Left Guard: Pull out behind tackle. Be prepared to pick up weakside outside linebacker should he rush. If not, help tackle or pick up inside rush with center.

Center: Odd front—step to left—be alert to pick up inside linebacker should he run through. If not, help right guard on nose tackle. Even front—step to left to pick up defensive tackle.

Right Guard: Odd front—drive down on nose tackle. Even front—block defensive tackle over you.

Right Tackle: Semi-aggressive block on defensive end. Be able to control him on line of scrimmage.

Fullback: Even front—drive through aggressively to pick up middle linebacker. Odd front—drive through aggressively to pick up inside linebacker. In either case, should linebacker move away, drift to 5 and 8 yards deep as an outlet for the quarterback (Diagram 9-24).

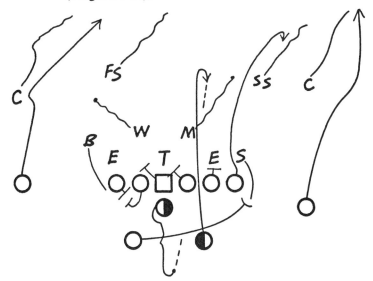

Diagram 9-24

Halfback: Make good fake of sweep toward strongside outside linebacker. Drive toward linebacker, coming under control to set up. Do

not block aggressively. The setup pass protection allows time to
pick up the rush which gives the quarterback adequate time to
deliver the pass.

Quarterback: Reverse out—fake ball to halfback—continue drop to complete seven steps. Before setting up, get head around to pick
up tight end. Be alert to adjust to coverage.

The bootleg action from the sweep is the other pass that has been highly
effective over the years. A quarterback with quickness and some running ability
can make this play into an exciting development (Diagram 9-25).

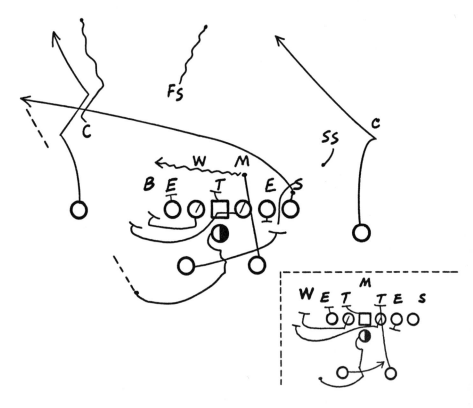

Diagram 9-25

Assignments for Bootleg Pass

Left End: Run deep corner pattern.

Left Tackle: Control-block defensive end.

Left Guard: Pull out left, get depth on second step. Be alert to pick up
weakside outside linebacker. If outside containment does not
rush, set outside left tackle for added protection.

Center: Versus odd front—block nose tackle—use control technique. Versus even front—reach-block weakside defensive tackle.

Right Guard: Pull out left—get depth on second step. Be alert to pick up weakside linebacker in odd front should he run through or should the middle linebacker in the even front run through. If the linebacker does not run upfield, continue outside the left guard for added protection.

Right Tackle: Set and block defensive end. Do not overcommit. Control-block after rush developments.

Tight End: Release inside across field gaining depth of 12 yards. Be alert to catch pass behind inside linebackers should they run through. If covered man-to-man, gain separation from coverage.

Flanker: Run post route.

Fullback: Versus odd front, drive toward strong inside linebacker and block aggressively. Should the linebacker not threaten, slide in front of linebackers toward weakside sideline as an outlet.

Halfback: Same as strongside sweep pass.

Quarterback: Reverse out—fake ball to halfback—place ball on far hip and roll left. Pick up Air Option principle in coverage with split end, tight end, and fullback. Be alert to dump ball early to tight end should a linebacker run through.

Trap Action

The trap action with the fake to the fullback and the pulling right guard prevents an unbelievable holding action on inside linebackers and offers a variety of pass pattern opportunities. It is feasible to develop many of the Air Option dropback patterns, combinations, or individual routes to either the weak side or strong side. In Diagram 9-26, the action illustrates one pattern that proved successful over the years.

The quarterback faces out toward the fullback, dropping back five steps. Because of the timing of the pattern, the quarterback makes only a hand-fake to the fullback. Because of this action, the quarterback is able to keep his eyes downfield to read the coverages. This is the reason it is possible to design almost any pattern in the Air Option notebook. The split end on the weak side runs a seven-step (10 yards) circle or turn-in pattern. The passing lane develops inside the weak outside linebacker. The faking action of the fullback holds the inside linebackers. The halfback drives toward the weakside linebacker and blocks him should he rush. If he hangs or drops off the line, the halfback drives toward the flat as an outlet.

The tight end releases inside and drives the middle to pull the free safety deep. The flanker runs an out route on the strong side for a one-on-one pattern should the coverages dictate to the quarterback to move his direction to the strong

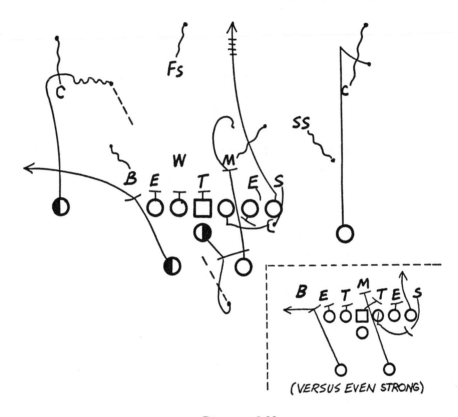

Diagram 9-26

side. The fullback blocks the inside linebacker versus the odd spacing, and the middle linebacker versus the even. Should the linebacker drop, the fullback should drift to a depth of 5 to 8 yards and turn out as an outlet. However, his faking action into the line of scrimmage is the most important part of his assignment. His action must affect the inside linebacker on the weakside.

Assignments

Left Tackle: Semi-aggressive block defensive end.

Left Guard: Versus even front—block defensive tackle. Versus odd front—be alert to pick up inside linebacker should he run through.

Center: Versus even front—block defensive tackle on strongside. Versus odd spacing—block nose tackle.

Right Guard: Pull out to right to pick up strong outside linebacker should he rush. If linebacker drops off the line, set up to help tackle.

Right Tackle: Block the defensive end aggressively but under control.

Draw Action

The draw action pass from the "I" formation can be one of the most effective of the play action series. In the Air Option attack, the draw (running) play is normally called on early downs. Therefore, the surprise element of throwing from this action is considered in an early down situation. A particularly successful situation is second and long (5 or more yards). The draw action pass sequence is easy to teach with a sound blocking scheme.

As in other play action passes, it is possible to utilize practically all of the Air Option passing game. The pattern in Diagram 9-27 was one of our favorites. The quarterback drops back the same as his regular dropback technique. As he is passing the halfback, driving into the line, the quarterback gives a hand-fake to the halfback and continues to drop until he reaches seven steps. His eyes stay downfield to read the coverages. The read is strictly the inside linebacker on the strong side in the odd-spacing defensive front or the middle linebacker in the even-spacing.

The pattern depends on the tight end to clear out the deep free safety. The combination is then set up between the flanker (wide receiver) running a crossing route across the middle at 15 to 18 yards, and the halfback driving into the line.

The faking halfback is the key to this particular masterpiece. He steps to his right one step, then drives toward his right guard. His fake must hold the inside

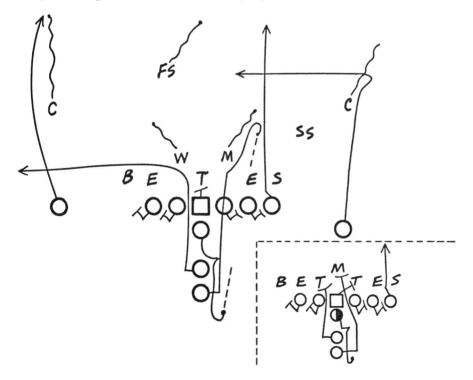

Diagram 9-27

linebackers momentarily, and simultaneously he must be alert to pick up the linebacker should he blitz. If the linebacker (strong inside linebacker, odd spacing—middle linebacker, even spacing) drops off the line to cover the pass, the halfback then becomes a receiver. His assignment is to get through the line without bumping either the center or the right guard off their blocks and set downfield 5 to 7 yards, hooking in front of the linebacker. This gives the quarterback a clean read. Should the linebacker jump the halfback, the quarterback stays with the Air Option principle and delivers to the crossing flanker. However, should the linebacker drop deep in front of the crossing deep pattern, the quarterback dumps the ball to the halfback (Diagram 9-27).

On the weak side, a combination pattern can be deployed with the split receiver and the fullback. Almost any individual route can be given to the split end to execute (Diagram 9-28).

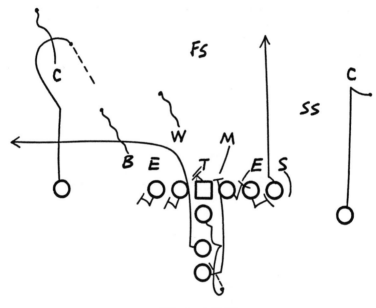

Diagram 9-28

On the snap, the fullback moves one step to the left and then drives into the line for his blocking assignment. Versus odd spacing, he picks up the weak inside linebacker; versus the even spacing, he is responsible for the defensive tackle. Should his linebacker responsibility drop off into coverage, his assignment includes breaking to the sideline as indicated in Diagram 9-28.

Interior Blocking Assignments

Left Tackle: Turn out on weakside linebacker.
Left Guard: Turn out on defensive end.

Center: Versus odd front—block nose tackle. Versus even front—block
    defensive tackle on right side.

Right Guard: Turn out on defensive end.

Right Tackle: Turn out on strongside linebacker.

Option Pass Action Sequence

Through the many years of the Air Option offense, the running game
consisted of several theories: from the Split-T, Belly series, Power Attack—
"knock them off the line" philosophy, the explosive Short-T (Parker Publishing
Co., Inc., 1962), Sweep-Trap Series, to the Triple Option (*Homer Rice on Triple
Option Football*, Parker Publishing Co., Inc., 1973). As we look back over the
years, it is evident the option or finesse style dominated our thinking. During the
closing years of my career (Homer Rice), we were working on an option pass
sequence. The result in Diagram 9-29 developed after years of experimentation.
Unfortunately, the option pass action does not have a track record because of the
late development. However, the concept is being presented here for the inno-
vative and creative thinking football coach who can see the many positive possi-
bilities.

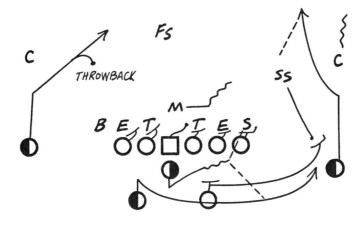

Diagram 9-29

The first stage of the option pass starts with the three-step dropback pass
action and finishes with a down-the-line pass-pitch or keep (Air Option Triple).

The quarterback quickly drops back three steps. As he hits on his third step
(under control), he drives toward the strong linebacker's inside shoulder. As he
moves down-the-line, his read focuses on the coverage in the seam between the
outside linebacker and the cornerback. If his "read" registers open lane, he will
drill the ball to the wide receiver (flanker) running a tight, short post route. If the
lane is closed, the quarterback executes the pitch-keep portion of the play. He has

the option to pitch to the trailing halfback or jump upfield with the keeper. Although the quarterback threatens the outside linebacker, he is being control-blocked by the tight end.

The halfback and fullback take one step toward the inside linebackers to delay one count ("one-thousand-one"), then swing to the right in the true option flow with the fullback running the arc as the lead blocker and the halfback trailing on his outside hip.

The split end (wide receiver on left) runs a slant route for a throwback potential when the inside linebackers and free safety desert their areas.

It's important for the flanker to push off the line of scrimmage for five steps before breaking tight to the inside into the open seam.

Blocking Assignments

Left Tackle: Set protection on defensive end.

Left Guard: Versus odd spacing, step toward linebacker. If he is close enough—block him, if he moves off—clip the nose tackle's heels. Versus even front—set protection on defensive tackle.

Center: Versus odd front—aggressively block nose tackle. Versus even front—check middle linebacker. If he does not rush, block aggressively to strongside.

Right Guard: Versus odd front—step toward and check-block linebacker. Should he move away, pull out behind tackle and tight end to lead-block for the quarterback.

Right Tackle: Aggressively block defensive end.

Tight End: Control-block strong linebacker. Do not lose him to inside. Should he drop off the line, turn inside to help right tackle.

Although your supplement package should be only 25 percent of your Air Option attack, your experience and talent on hand may dictate its usage. Several coaches have taken the principle of the Air Option package and rearranged the techniques into their own thinking, whether it be dropback, sprint-out, roll-out, pull-up, or other action sequences. There are many ways to accomplish the end result. The "point" is—establish a sound plan and utilize the correct teaching procedures with correct practice, practice, practice. Let the "mind" soar, and enjoy your beliefs.

Chapter 10

GAME

PLANNING

PLANNING for the big game is the most intriguing experience the coach encounters. Preparation involves several areas.

Planning starts first with gaining vital information on your opponent. The responsibilities are divided into three areas. The defensive coordinator and his staff prepare a report on the opponent's offense. The special team's coach puts together information on the kicking game. The offensive coordinator and his staff organize the report regarding the opponent's defensive tendencies. The head coach then must plan a program for the week to adequately teach and prepare the squad for the upcoming game. His leadership must also provide motivation to prepare the team to play on game day.

This chapter will deal primarily with information on preparing the Air Option Offense for an upcoming contest. In devising a plan for the Air Option, we followed a checklist to put together a complete report. We started first with the running game. Through scouting our opponent and film study, we broke the points of interest down into seven categories: 1) Defensive Basic Fronts, 2) Stunts, 3) Force, 4) Personnel, 5) Short-Yardage Fronts, 6) Goal-Line Fronts, and 7) Prevent Fronts.

1) *Basic Fronts* were sorted into down and distance categories: first and ten, second and long (7 or more yards), second and medium (3 to 6 yards), third and long (5 or more yards), third and medium (3 to 4 yards).

If the coach is fortunate enough to have access to a computer system, he will save valuable time. After the computer is programmed for all the ''needs,'' it requires only minutes to compile a report.

141

The fronts varied from week to week. A front involves the spacing of down linemen—even, odd, stacked, over- or undershifted. The fronts determine the blocking schemes to be utilized by our offensive linemen for our selected running plays and for protection in our passing game.

Then the basic fronts are checked by formation. Some fronts will shift toward a certain type of formation strength or shift away to fit into a type of secondary coverage. This sometimes can be a tip for the quarterback.

It is important for the quarterback to understand the basic fronts. He will be instructed that on certain called plays when a particular front appears, he should audible another designated play. It serves two vital purposes for the quarterback. He can audible out of a play to prevent a bad call, and he can audible to a play that can take advantage of a certain front and result in a big play.

2) *Stunts* are sorted by down and distance and by formation. This again presents the quarterback with a tip for strategy purposes if a linebacker or down lineman's alignment indicates a stunt is coming. Stunts have another important element—stunts by field position. Some defensive units have a distinct tendency to stunt in certain areas of the field. Knowing of a strong tendency in a particular area is an advantage in staying out of particular calls or taking advantage of a stunt for a big play.

Organization of your opponent's stunts also allows the offensive line coach to determine blocking schemes, pickups, and pass protections.

The field position for stunts is broken down into four critical areas:

1. Inside −10 (backed up)
2. +20
3. +10
4. Inside +4 (going in)

These areas can make or break the offense. A bad play backed up inside the minus-10 yard line will in all probability give the opponent favorable field position. A bad play from the plus-20 yard line to the goal line will stop a potential score which could cost the total game. Big losses in these critical areas are difficult to make up.

3) *Force* pertains to rotation of the secondary coverage to a running play regardless of alignment versus a formation. There are three basic coverages to both the strong and weak side: roll-up (Diagram 10-1), invert (Diagram 10-2), man-to-man (Diagram 10-3).

Although there are many types of combinations mixed with these coverages, understanding the basic force or outside containment versus the run allows the offense to utilize certain arrangements to dictate to the defense what they can employ from the basic maneuvers.

The perimeter coverages are studied to determine if there is a way to control or limit the coverages by splitting the wide receivers to a designated

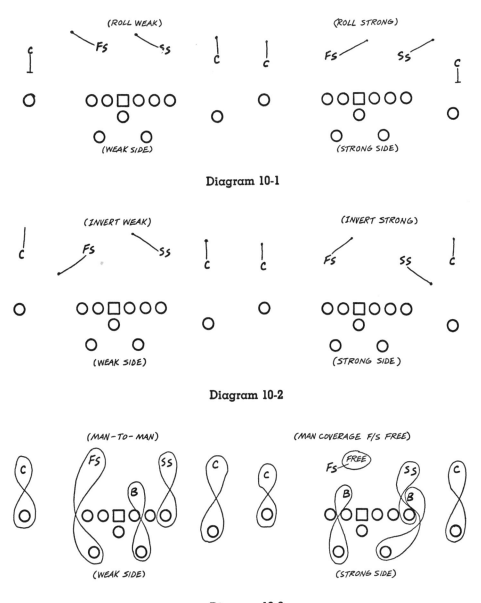

Diagram 10-1

Diagram 10-2

Diagram 10-3

width, by motion, or any type of unusual alignment. By restricting the defensive coverages, an offensive plan will have more opportunities to exploit its strength.

Therefore, the offensive plan is mapped out each week after the facts are in on the effect our formations, spacing, and use of motion will have versus the opponent's force.

Other considerations must be covered regarding outside linebackers and defensive ends. When a play develops, who trails from the backside, the

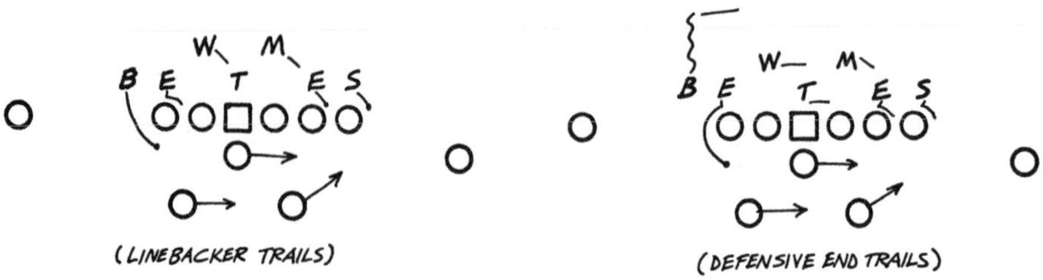

(LINEBACKER TRAILS)   (DEFENSIVE END TRAILS)

Diagram 10-4

linebacker or the defensive end (Diagram 10-4)? This is important to determine for reverses, cutbacks, and backside traps.

By understanding "force," the quarterback can detect any tips the coverage may render regarding down and distance, and field position to the running game.

4) *Personnel* study in a scouting report can provide the winning edge. Tom Landry of the Dallas Cowboys and Lou Holtz of Minnesota are masters in preparing a team for the big game. Their thought preparations have kept them on top.

First, study the defensive linemen. Do they exercise read penetration or close technique? Again, the offensive line coach will need the information to teach the proper blocking technique. Next, compile information on the linebackers regarding their alignment, how they attack a play, are they soft versus a run? Particularly check the middle or inside linebackers on their movement down the line. Do they flow with the play or fill? The type of technique employed by each defender on the line of scrimmage is important to understand before a running game plan can be put together.

After the techniques are established, attention moves to individual characteristics. Defensive linemen are vulnerable to some area of the game. If their individual weakness can be detected, the design of a play can become an advantage. Starting with a straight-ahead play, search for the soft areas. Normally, a linebacker who plays too deep off the line is a good target. Some linemen are good pursuers when the ball is directed away from them but cannot handle an attack head-on. It is vital to be able to pick out these characteristics. The next point-of-attack is running wide. Which corner is vulnerable to a wide sweep or option? Then we analyze for the trap. Who is the hard charging lineman? Can he be trapped? (See Diagram 10-5.)

Next, we approach the draw play versus the hard rusher in the passing game. In Diagram 10-6, the defensive end rushes the passer hard and outside. He is vulnerable to the draw.

One other characteristic is the "give it." This play can gain valuable yardage if used sparingly versus the "reading" defensive lineman (Diagram 10-7). The defensive tackle is left unblocked. If he follows or closes with the trapping guard, he opens a running lane for a big play.

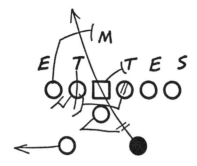

(DEFENSIVE TACKLE CHARGES UPFIELD)

Diagram 10-5

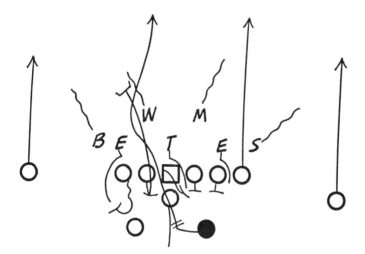

Diagram 10-6

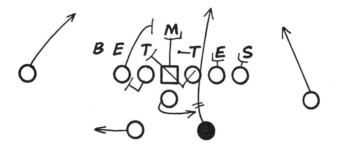

Diagram 10-7

5) *Short Yardage* situations are critical in every game. Making the first down in these situations—third down with 2 yards or less to go (fourth down—2 yards or less in 4 down zone) will keep the drive going and give the offense future opportunities to score. Therefore, it is imperative to study carefully the defensive alignment and charge, and then determine the areas to attack. Select three or four plays for the game, execute them perfectly. Occasionally, it is possible to pick out a big play on a short yardage situation. Study personnel characteristics in Diagram 10-8. The weakside corner rotates on a flat course in

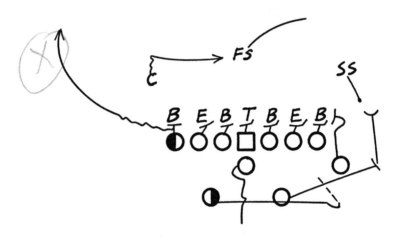

Diagram 10-8

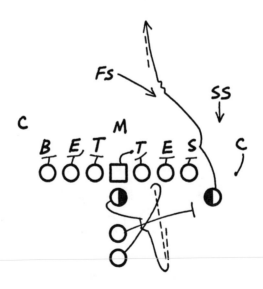

Diagram 10-9

reacting to a wide play to the strongside. He is vulnerable to the old halfback throwback pass to a delayed end. The offensive end must delay five counts.

A free safety who fills fast on an inside run is vulnerable to the closed flanker slipping through the middle. After the handoff, the deep back takes two steps toward the line of scrimmage and pivots back with a toss to the quarterback. The closed flanker must fake a block on the free safety before he slips by him (Diagram 10-9).

6) *Goal-Line Fronts* are determined inside the plus-5 yard line. The offensive line coach will study carefully the alignment and characteristics for the running game and recommend three or four runs. This is not a time to experiment. The offense must cash in on this opportunity. The defense normally brings in an extra lineman substituting for a linebacker or secondary defender. If the situation becomes third down with 3 or more yards to go, the defense in all probability will take the extra lineman out, returning the secondary man for a possible passing situation. It is important to understand the defensive strategy at this moment.

The six-five front is the basic goal line defense employed by many teams (Diagram 10-10).

The three-four walked-up front is also a widely used goal line front (Diagram 10-11).

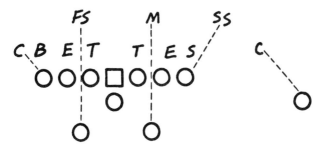

Diagram 10-10

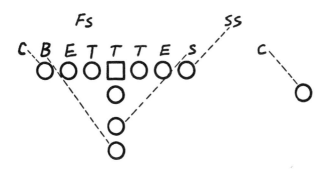

Diagram 10-11

Later in this chapter under the passing game versus goal line defenses, we will go into greater detail and give you several scoring plays that have been highly successful through the years for the Air Option offense.

After the running attack plan is set, we move to the passing game. The passing game covers 17 categories: 1) coverages by down and distance, 2) coverages by field position, 3) coverages by formation, 4) coverage tips correlated with our check-with-me and audible system, 5) blitz, 6) secondary adjustment versus twin set (two wide receivers to formation—tight-end opposite), 7) secondary adjustment to motion, effect on force, coverage, blitz, linebacker reaction, 8) personnel, 9) underneath coverage tendencies, 10) tight end release effect on coverage, 11) +20 yard line to +11 yard line, 12) +10 yard line to +4 yard line, 13) goal line (+4 to goal line), 14) short yardage, 15) two minutes, 16) nickel coverages, 17) prevent defense.

Studying each of these areas develops the plan-of-action. Going into the game fully prepared takes the guesswork and "grab bag" tactics out of coaching on game day. When a team utilizes a surprise tactic, it is much easier to adjust to if you have covered all the areas previously.

In the 1950's, Coach Don Fouss, of East Orange High School in New Jersey and later of Purdue University, put together a book, "Quarterback Generalship". Don's book laid out the basic plans to train the quarterback and the coach on a game strategy. His concept was widely absorbed at that time by many of our top coaches. I also benefited by studying the book in detail and developing the system in this chapter.

1) *Coverages by down and distance:* Coverages are charted and broken down into these categories:

First and 10 yards to go

Second and 7 or more

Second and 3 to 6

Second and 1 to 6

Third and 6 or more

Third and 3 to 5

Third and 2 or less

If the opponent has a certain tendency on any of the down-and-distance categories, it helps in planning the type of patterns you will employ on those specific situations. For example, one opponent had a high-percentage tendency of always utilizing a weakside invert coverage on first and 10 (Diagram 10-12). Diagram 10-13 illustrates one of the first and 10 patterns we put together in preparation for a big play on first down.

As you work with your passing game versus the opponent's down-and-distance tendencies, you are able to develop the type of patterns that fit into the various situations. This is a tremendous "tool" for the quarterback and the press box coach to determine a plan by situation.

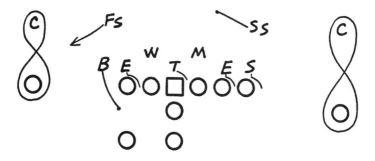

Diagram 10-12

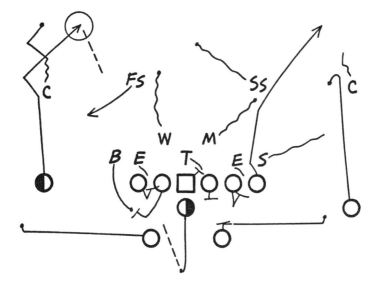

Diagram 10-13

2) *Coverage by field position:* The critical areas to chart regarding field positions are:

a. Goal line to −9 yard line (backed up)

b. −10 to +21

c. +20 to +11

d. +10 to +5

e. +4 to goal line

Some teams have strong tendencies regarding their coverages in relation to the position the ball is on the field. The most damaging area is the backed-up area—goal line to the minus-9 yard line. When the defense forces a turnover or a punt out of the end zone, it nearly always gives your opponent excellent field position which can change the complexion of the game.

The first rule when you're coming off your own goal line is to get the ball to the 5-yard line to prevent punting out of the end zone from tight punt formation. Failure to move to the 5-yard line forces a quicker kick and prevents the linemen from adequate coverage on the return.

The next plan should be a play that has an opportunity to give you a big play and move the ball well upfield. Nothing is more discouraging to the defense than the offense escaping from their own goal line. It is advisable not to play the game in your backyard.

A play pass pattern that proved reliable over a period of years in Diagram 10-14 can result in the big play and turn the game around completely.

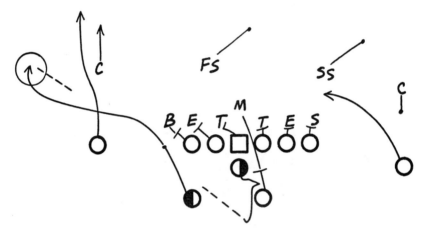

Diagram 10-14

The halfback drives toward the linebacker until the offensive left tackle engages the linebacker. The halfback then breaks outside and up the side line. This is an excellent first and 10 call when backed up. However, we must emphasize, move the ball to the 5-yard line. Run the quarterback sneak with wedge blocking to achieve spread punt formation punting spacing.

3) *Coverage by formation:* Be sure to check the films for coverages versus different types of formations. There may be a tip that the defense employs certain coverages versus certain formations. The advantage to gain in the passing game is to limit the defense to as few coverages as possible. If a certain formation locks the defense to a definite coverage, then the offense has an advantage. Knowing where they are and their intentions before the snap, can enhance the security every coach would like to possess.

4) *Coverage tips:* Can we utilize check-with-me or audible? Check the safeties for depth and/or width. For certain coverages, they align deeper or wider. This can be an important tip. When it is analyzed, can you audible to get

to a particular pass pattern or can you go to the line of scrimmage (check-with-me) and call the pattern on the line after recognizing the tip? Another tip is to recognize whether the safety is looking at a particular receiver or is he looking at the quarterback. When he "eyeballs" a receiver, he is in man coverage—looking at the quarterback means he is playing zone.

Next, check the corners. They give the most tips. Throughout my coaching career, I have found more tips from the characteristics of corner play than any other position. Always check their depth. They are taught to play a certain depth on certain coverages. Most corners will get a little lower and look at the receiver when in man coverages. When in zone, they have a tendency to stand taller and look in toward the quarterback. Their width also is a tip. If they are outside the wide receivers, they will be in zone coverage. Inside a wide receiver means always man coverage if he looks at the receivers. If he is inside and looks in toward the line of scrimmage, he is coming on a corner stunt.

Linebackers also are big "tippers." Their alignment indicates their intentions once you have studied their characteristics in your film study.

5) *Blitz:* In recording the defensive blitz in your scouting reports, you will be able to associate the blitz by down and distance, field position, formation, and fronts. Most defensive coaches have strong tendencies regarding their blitz.

It is wise to list their blitz as 1-2-3, etc., with the most effective being in that order—1-2-3. Some teams we have played in the past had strong tendencies on third and long. Others were categorized by field position such as in our plus-20 yard line zone.

There is an old saying in the National Football League, "If you live by the blitz, you will die by the blitz." Ken Anderson, our quarterback with the Cincinnati Bengals, was a master in picking up the blitz for a big play. This came about because Ken spent many hours studying film after film of the opponent's blitzes. We always broke our film down into various areas. One film was isolated on the opponent's blitz by situation. The Pittsburgh Steelers, during their great World Championship years, were intimidating with their many blitzes. One particular week in preparation for the Steelers, Ken Anderson put in "overtime" on that particular reel of film on the Steeler's blitzes. We had six big plays in the game as a result of this planning to beat the Steelers 34-10, the worst defeat during their great years.

Some teams will walk up and bluff a blitz and move out of it when they force you to audible or change protection schemes. Snapping the ball on a quick count and reading their coverage after the snap can be highly effective.

Diagrams 10-15 and 10-16 indicate wide receivers must break to the inside when the safety on their side blitzes.

Another method to control a safety blitz is to put the back on the blitz side in motion. Motion either takes the blitz off or gives the offense an easy option to read. (See Diagram 10-17.)

Many blitz alignments result in inside-out man coverage by the corners. The outside deep routes are always there when the receiver "sticks" the defender to the inside on a post move. (See Diagram 10-18.)

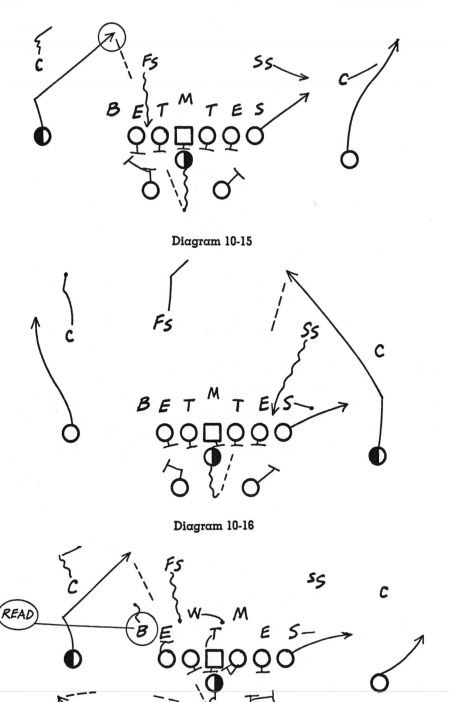

Diagram 10-15

Diagram 10-16

Diagram 10-17

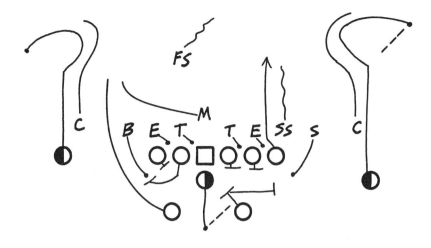

Diagram 10-18

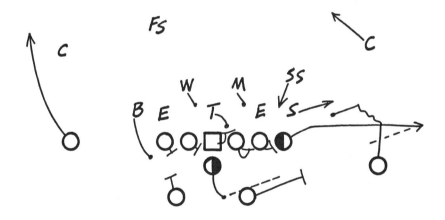

Diagram 10-19

Beating a blitz is preplanned. Recognize the type of blitz and have a pattern to take advantage. The important fact is "do not be intimidated."

In Diagram 10-19, the strongside safety gives away a man coverage with an all-out rush. The tight end picks it up and releases to the flat. The flanker breaks back to the inside and crosses in front of the strong linebacker, serving as a screen. The quarterback is able to dump the ball to the tight end for a big play.

6) *Secondary adjustment versus twin set:* One of our favorite formations through the years was the twin set (Cincinnati formation). The twin set puts the two wide receivers wide to the formation side, and the tight end splits to the opposite side (Diagram 10-20).

The twin set forces the secondary to adjust to the two wide receivers on one side. It gives the offense an opportunity to select one defender and isolate a particular receiver in his zone.

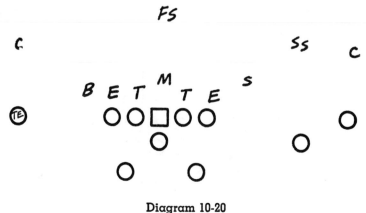

Diagram 10-20

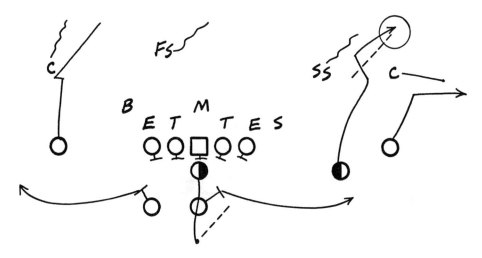

Diagram 10-21

When a switch is made (both wide receivers on one side— tight end opposite), it is imperative to know how the secondary will handle the three wide receivers. Some will play their same coverages. This means the strong safety may end up man-to-man on a wide receiver. Sometimes this can be to the offense's advantage if there is a difference in speed. Most defensive coaches line up their slowest defender at strong safety. Take advantage of a mismatch. (See Diagram 10-21.)

Some teams will keep the corners with the two wide receivers and switch the strong safety to a corner to cover the tight end. This is a time to have a substitution ready to exploit speed at the tight end position versus the strong safety. (See Diagram 10-22.) Don Bass at the University of Houston was a tight

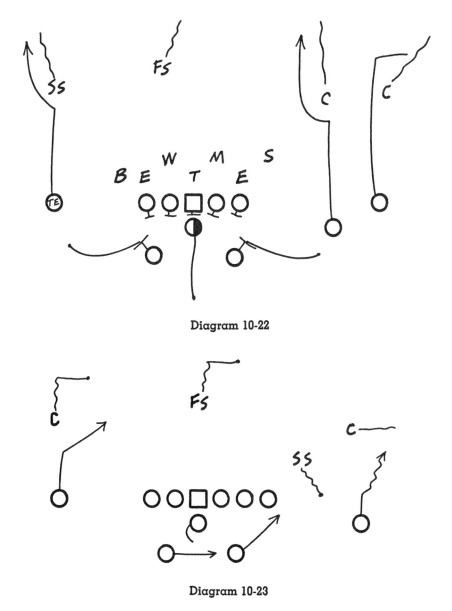

Diagram 10-22

Diagram 10-23

end with wide receiver speed. Don played for us at Cincinnati (Bengals), and when our opponent switched, Don was sent deep to outrun the strong safety.

7) *Secondary adjustment to motion:* Utilizing a man in motion after the offense sets a formation, has always intrigued me as to how the various secondaries will adjust. A formation establishes a strong side with its flanker. (See Diagram 10-23.) The secondary will adjust its coverage to the strength—and once the ball is snapped, they react with the called coverage to a run or pass.

   The next play the offense sets its formation with the flanker to determine strength. The secondary will adjust to the strength. Before the ball is snapped, the flanker crosses the formation in motion which changes the strength to the opposite side. (See Diagram 10-24.)

   The defense must readjust its coverage to the strength on the opposite side. There are three basic ways a secondary coverage will adjust. In Diagram 10-25, the secondary simply rolls its coverage. This coverage puts the strong safety in centerfield.

   The second method is to run the strong safety across the formation, which does not change responsibility. (See Diagram 10-26.)

   The third method is the corner staying with the flanker, which in most cases indicates a man-to-man coverage. (See Diagram 10-27.)

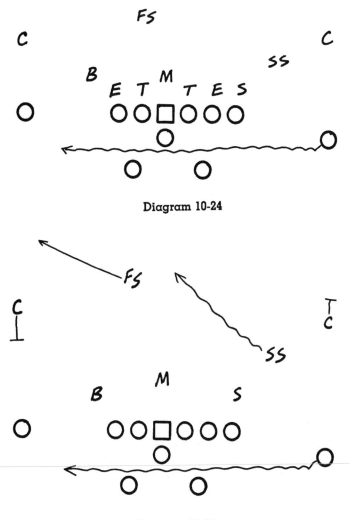

Diagram 10-24

Diagram 10-25

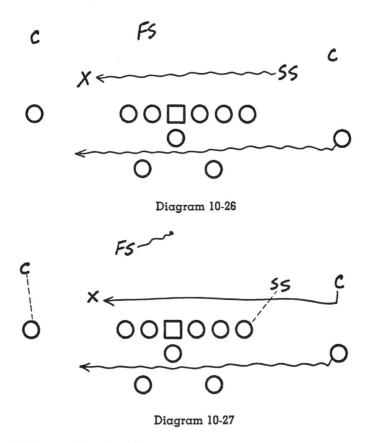

Diagram 10-26

Diagram 10-27

8) *Personnel study* of the defensive coverage is important to determine strengths and weaknesses of each individual. Study each defender for these characteristics: On big play possession downs—can we get him out of position in switch or motion, how does he react to play action or a pump fake?

9) *Underneath coverage tendencies.* Study of the underneath coverage is important for screen and delay routes. For screens, determine type and direction, down and distance, field position, and any problems with defensive line.

Delay routes versus zone coverages are trouble for the defense, particularly if the linebackers drop deep into the coverage.

10) *Tight end release* effect on coverage is important to determine because a coverage may be predicted by the tight end's release. The strong safety reacts differently to an inside release than he does to an outside release. (See Diagram 10-28.) If the tight end's release will have an effect on the coverage, it presents the offense another tool with which to operate and control the coverage.

11) *Plus-20 yard line to plus-11 yard line.* Here's the area where the offense should strike. First, record the opponent's tendencies in the area involving their coverages, blitz, tips, and the personnel to attack. Then map out a strategy involving your passing game that will exploit the defense's coverage, blitz, and tips. Most importantly, search out the personnel to attack in this area.

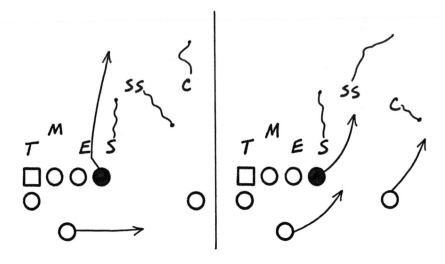

Diagram 10-28

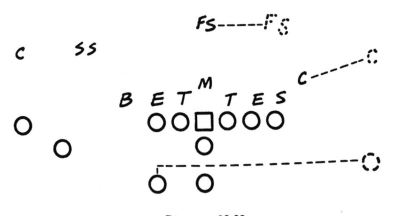

Diagram 10-29

Through the years, we were most successful in this area because the defense has strong tendencies in this situation. One particular scheme we continued to revert back to was the twin-flanker formation (Diagram 10-29) because of its high rate of success.

The halfback sprints to a flanker position on the quarterback's command (after the offense aligns on the line of scrimmage) and sets. This allows time for the secondary to adjust. The key for direction is the free safety. If the area safety remains in centerfield, the pattern is called to the right side with the tight end and flanker. Should the free safety move over the tight end, the pattern goes to the twin side.

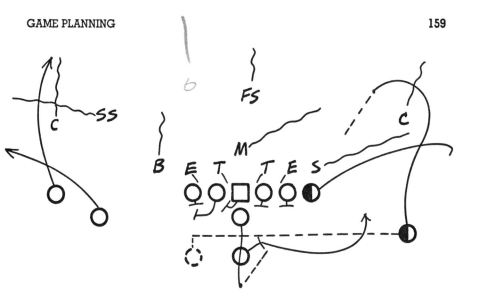

Diagram 10-30

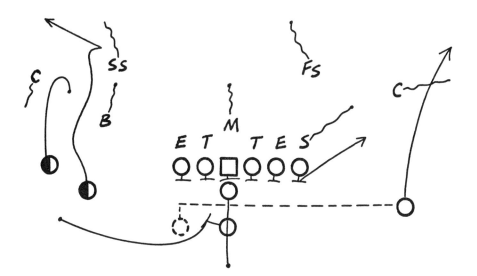

Diagram 10-31

Diagram 10-30 indicates the free safety remaining in centerfield. Diagram 10-31 reveals the free safety adjusting to the tight-end side which checks the pattern to the twin set.

This scheme is simple to employ, but it is imperative to show the formation with the halfback at home base before running him to a flanker position. Several

Air Option patterns can be designed for either direction from this formation. Sometimes we substitute a wide receiver for the halfback in this situation.

12) *Plus 10 to plus 5 and*

13) *Plus 4 to goal line* are the exciting going-in-to score areas. The areas are split from +10 to +4 and +4 to the goal line because of the substitution factor. When does the defense bring in the extra lineman? Most defensive coaches send in the down lineman for a secondary man inside the 5-yard line. Both areas must be evaluated for coverages, blitz, tips, and personnel to attack.

Through the years, the Air Option offense has enjoyed phenomenal success. One year at Rice University with quarterback Tommy Kramer at the helm, we failed to score only once inside the 10-yard line during the entire season.

Much credit must go to the emphasis put on this segment of the game. Through the years I have watched teams move the ball down the field but fail to put any points on the scoreboard. Several years ago, Jerry Claiborne, one of the top collegiate coaches, lectured at the clinic on the importance of goal-line defense. In fact, he placed emphasis on this part of the game by beginning the practice each day with live contact goal-line defense. This influenced my thinking to do the same offensively. Therefore, each day we spent the first period of organized practice with "live" goal-line offense. This period was not only good for our goal-line offense and defense but got everyone's attention early in practice. It turned out to be a stimulator for the rest of the practice.

Strategy for the going-in attack was determined on the yard line the first down occurred. First and goal on the 10-yard line was a passing down. First and goal inside the 5-yard line was a running down. However, because of our confidence in the throwing game, we believed we could "throw it" in on any down or situation.

The following pattern in Diagram 10-32 was one of the successful scoring passes utilized for the scoring attack. The key is the weakside linebacker. When the weakside linebacker rushes, the ball is dumped off to the fullback swinging wide to the weak side. If the weakside linebacker drops off to the outside to cover the fullback, the quarterback reverts back to the wide receiver from the weak side crossing near the end line for an opening. Should the wide receiver be tightly covered, the ball must be thrown over his head to prevent a possible interception.

The under-route had the highest scoring rate of any pattern in the going-in attack (Diagram 10-33). The details must be adhered to completely for its success. The wide receiver must sprint quickly off the line and then slow down under control, waiting for the inside receiver (tight end) to drive between the defensive cornerback and the wide receiver. When the inside receiver reaches the inside screen position, the wide receiver must break underneath to the inside and look immediately for the ball from the quarterback. The tight end should continue to the corner of the end zone, stop, and turn out. Should the defensive strong safety pull up inside, the tight end becomes free for the outlet. Should the outside linebacker cover outside, he leaves open the path of the fullback in the

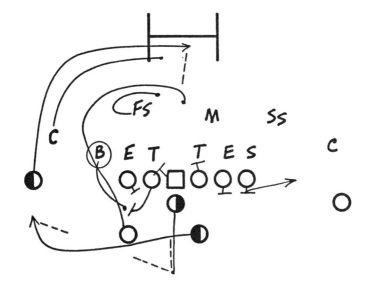

Diagram 10-32

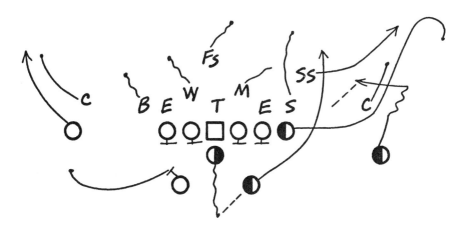

Diagram 10-33

seam. We always preferred our quarterback to backpedal on this route in order to stop, plant, and release the ball as the progression develops. The under-pattern was executed with flexibility. In Diagram 10-34 motion is used to exploit the pattern to the weak side.

The zip play action pattern in Diagram 10-35 was another highly consistent scoring pattern. This is an excellent first and goal call. The zip play action pattern is a one-man pattern. The pass is strictly a "feel" between the quarterback and

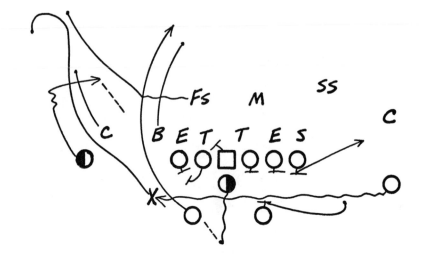

Diagram 10-34

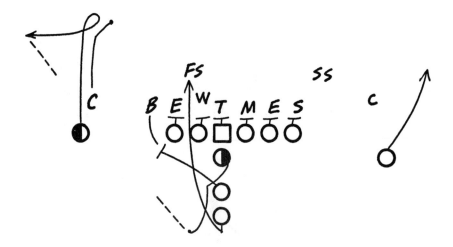

Diagram 10-35

the receiver. The execution of the receiver is the key. He must sprint off the line, taking an outside release, and drive into the end zone before making the curl move inside. As he curls inside, he must plant his inside foot and pivot to the outside, with his eyes on the ball releasing from the quarterback. The quarterback makes a good fake to his deep back, sets, and releases the ball to the outside when the receiver plants his inside foot. If executed properly, the pattern is almost impossible to stop.

The zip pattern can be thrown to either side (wide receiver) or to the tight end as shown in Diagram 10-36.

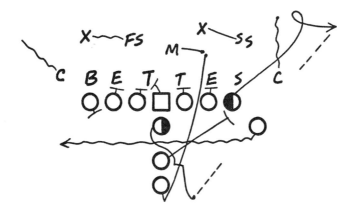

Diagram 10-36

There were other patterns in the going-in-attack (step-and-go, tight end drag, fullback flat, and others), but through the years the weakside flood, under, and zip patterns always rated high on the consistency list. However, I must emphasize again, we started practice each day with a ten-minute, "live" goal-line scoring (going-in-attack) period. The importance of this period pays handsome dividends.

14) *Short yardage* was covered in the running game because 98 percent of the time this is a running down. The 2 percent is for the special pattern picked out in film study as indicated in this study.

15) *The two-minute offense* is another segment in the offense that must be practiced daily. As mentioned previously, we always began our formal practice with a ten-minute, "live" contact goal-line offensive period. Conversely, we always closed practice with a ten-minute "two-minute" drill. Each day we would give the quarterback a different situation: the score, time-outs left, time left in the game, weather conditions, noise factor, and yard line. The quarterback took the situations under advisement and began to work with no huddle, check-with-me, stopping the clock, calling time-outs, and scoring a touchdown or positioning for a field-goal attempt. We could write another book on this section alone, but let us emphasize the importance of utilizing your two-minute offense in practice daily. In 1968, at the University of Cincinnati, quarterback Greg Cook was a master in operating the two-minute offense. We pulled several games out in the late stages, particularly a dramatic finish over Bo Schembechler's outstanding Miami team with three touchdowns in the late stages of the fourth quarter, plus a winning field goal (47 yards) by Jim O'Brien with three seconds left in the game. The two-minute attack becomes an awareness by the entire squad and coaching staff. The adrenalin must be flowing with electricity. Alertness to get out-of-bounds to stop the clock, to hurry up on the line, to hear the next play, when in a huddle to comprehend two plays called at once, and on and on.

With two minutes to play, behind by 6 points, on the minus-20 yard line, I felt confident we could score and take the lead with or without time-outs remaining. For one thing the defense normally sets in one coverage. Utilizing the Air Option attack with the principles explained in this manuscript can be highly productive and victorious. Our "thing" was to mix the sideline cuts, crossing routes, and delay dumps to perfection. Sideline cuts are almost always there because of the cushion the corners give in this situation. Once the ball is caught, the receiver gets as much yardage upfield as possible and then steps out-of-bounds to stop the clock. When a crossing or delay pass is caught, the team must be ready to sprint to the ball and receive the next play on the line of scrimmage. If it is necessary to stop the clock, the quarterback commands "clock-clock-clock," and on the first sound the quick-out pattern is executed by the wide receiver to the shortest side of the field whereby the quarterback can throw the football out-of-bounds.

Occasionally, a running play such as a draw or screen pass can be utilized in this drive. However, the quarterback must always be aware of the time left, and the number of downs. The cardinal sin is to call the "clock" play on fourth down.

When no time-outs are left, it is almost imperative to pass every down, and when the receiver does not get out-of-bounds, stop the clock.

The two-minute, no-huddle attack can become a strategic weapon. It can also be employed to start a game, or to start the second half, or be used at any point in the game as a surprise element. Keeping the defense from huddling can prevent the defense from changing fronts and coverages.

Once a week, we always had a short period to execute running out the clock. Games have been lost during this period because of a bad snap or a running play that caused a fumble. In Diagram 10-37, a safety is placed 10 yards behind the offense in the event a problem arises. The quarterback should take the

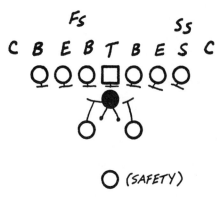

Diagram 10-37

ball and drop to the turf behind the line protecting the ball from slipping out. When the clock is running, utilize the maximum amount of allowed time before the snap.

16) *The nickel defense:* The nickel concept is a stratagem of the defense to substitute a fifth back for a linebacker when an obvious long-yardage passing situation develops. It gives the defense an extra secondary defender. In most cases, the defense will double the outside receivers. (See Diagram 10-38.,

We utilized a "read" principle that was extremely successful versus the fifth back arrangement. It is important in your scouting and film study to understand how the defense exploits the nickel principle. Most of our opponents mixed a zone and man coverage with this deployment. The "read" principle gave us the best attack regardless of their reaction.

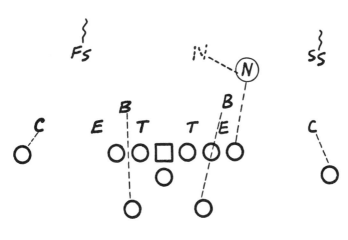

Diagram 10-38

In Diagram 10-39, the defense executes man coverage. They have tipped the coverage because of the corner's alignment. This pattern can be worked to either side. In Diagram 10-40, the quarterback has selected the left side (away from formation). The wide receiver releases outside on a "go" route, taking his coverage as deep as possible. The inside receiver, the halfback moved up in a slot position, releases outside and upfield for 12 yards. As he releases, he "reads" the cornerback. When the corner runs deep with the wide receiver, the halfback breaks to the sideline for the pass. Should the corner indicate a zone coverage in Diagram 10-40, the halfback sets down (12 yards deep) between the corner and the linebacker. This arrangement versus a "nickel" coverage produced results. The defense can't be right.

Careful study of your opponent's "nickel" will enable you to select several appropriate Air Option design patterns to counter the defensive specialties.

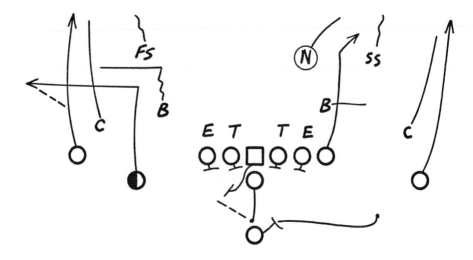

Diagram 10-39

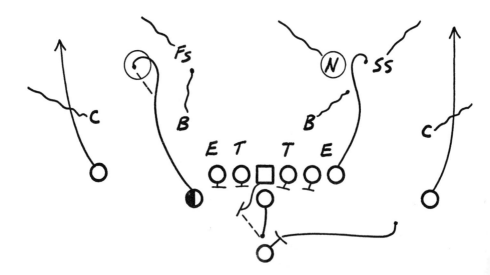

Diagram 10-40

17) *The Prevent Defense* is used by the opponent during the last series in a game to prevent a long pass that would lose the game with a score. Diagram 10-41 is the typical prevent defense. The defense covers the four short zones, the three deep zones, and, positions a secondary "trooper" 20 yards deep from the ball as a security measure should any zone break down.

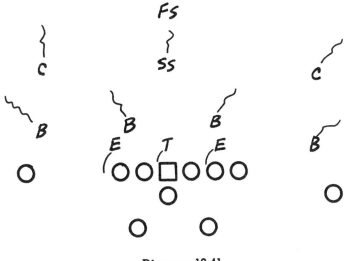

Diagram 10-41

The fallacy in a prevent defense is the three-man rush. The quarterback has time to drop back and find an open seam in the defense. From this our philosophy developed—take what they will give us and move the ball, stopping the clock as needed. Once you are able to move to the plus-30 yard line, the ''trooper'' stationed 20 yards deep is no longer a factor. The defense is now playing with ten defenders. This forces the defense to return to a basic defense but by now they have worked themselves into a ''soft'' concept becoming vulnerable to an aggressive offensive Air Option attack. At this point we were always prepared to return to our plus-20 yard line to goal line plan.

Game planning is an intricate phase of the Air Option. The point is— understand each area of operation, develop a plan for each situation, then apply perfect practice periods to teach and execute the plan.

SUMMARY OF

THE AIR OPTION

The Air Option passing game has been an exciting manuscript to prepare for the reader. The message will become clear that it is imperative for the football coach to understand the principles presented in this book before assembling the plan of action. We are convinced unless the principles are thoroughly understood, the coach, the player, and the fan are missing a segment of the game that is the difference—the winning game in the championship on any level—high school, collegiate, professional. In the Orange Bowl game, January 1, 1984, the University of Miami coached by Howard Schnellenberger defeated a University of Nebraska team ranked number one in the nation that many of the experts ranked as one of the greatest football teams in collegiate history. Howard Schnellenberger learned the passing game from Blanton Collier at the University of Kentucky many years ago. His refinement of this concept as Head Coach of the Baltimore Colts, as Offensive Coordinator of the Los Angeles Rams with George Allen and the Miami Dolphins under Don Schula, gave him the edge. His Miami team defeated this great University of Nebraska team with the Air Option passing principles to win the national championship. One year prior to that, Joe Paterno's Penn State team defeated a University of Georgia team boasting one of the greatest running backs of all time in Herschel Walker, by utilizing the dropback passing game with their fine quarterback, Todd Blackburn. Joe Paterno's teams have been in the final game many times, but not until the exploitation of these passing game principles was he able to win all the "marbles"—the national championship. These examples are plentiful on the high school level and professional level as well. For the football coach to implement the Air Option he must understand completely the details involving each element. Once this is understood, then it is important to adapt the individual skilled athletes to the game. We are not always blessed with a great quarterback or outstanding receivers. These individuals must be developed through the various training programs in practice periods described in the Air Option manuscript. Also, it is important to utilize the characteristics in different types of skills your quarterback and receivers possess. For example, if your quarterback is more adapted to the sprint-out passing game because of his great running ability, then this should be exploited—utilizing the principles of the Air Option attack. If the quarterback lacks the great arm, then it is important to adjust the passing routes with the step-count method to coordinate these deficiencies. All in all, it leaves the imagination of the coach with many options. One phase that cannot be overlooked are the offensive linemen up front who must protect the quarterback. Utilization of time to develop this area of the game must be adhered to before any of the other frills can be added. The signal should be clear. To win BIG, it is imperative to implement Air Option principles. When your opponent's personnel are physically stronger, the adoption of the Air Option will narrow the gap, providing an equality that cannot be obtained with a solo running game.

The information has been presented. The reader will be the benefactor. We hope you enjoy this stimulating concept.

INDEX